AWARD-WINNING RECIPES FROM ACROSS AMERICA

PERFECT FRUIT PIES

A Storey Publishing Book

Storey Communications, Inc.
Schoolhouse Road
Pownal, Vermont 05261

Front cover photograph from Stark Bro's Nurseries and Orchards
Front cover design and text design by Carol Jessop
Introductory material written by Glenn Andrews
Edited by Constance L. Oxley
Indexed by Kathleen D. Bagioni
Recipe consultant, Edith M. Stovel
Project editor, Gwen W. Steege

Printed in the United States by Courier
Fourth printing, November 1991

Library of Congress Cataloging-in-Publication Data

Perfect fruit pies : award-winning recipes from across America.
        p.   cm.
    "A Storey Publishing book."
    Includes index.
    ISBN 0-88266-638-X (hc) — ISBN 0-88266-647-9 (pb)
    1. Pies   2. Cookery (Fruit)   I. Storey Communications.
    TX773.P447   1990
    641.8'652—dc20   90-50418
                                CIP

Contents

INTRODUCTION

What could be more delicious than a fruit pie, a *perfect* fruit pie, juicy, full of flavor, with a just-right texture? Fruit pies are America's number-one desserts, no doubt about it. (In fact, in some parts of the country, they're also the classic favorite breakfast.) They're the stuff we dream of. "Home and Mom's apple pie" symbolized the end of World War II. Every small-restaurant counter contains a mouth-watering display of cherry, apple, peach, and berry pies. Even at the fanciest big-city restaurants, you'll usually find some sort of apple tart or other fruit pie creation being devoured by happy eaters in preference to the most elaborate chocolate confections. We love our fruit pies!

There's a lot of competition among fruit pie-makers. This shows up in county and state fairs, where the exhibitions of pickles, jams, and preserves pale beside the fruit pies. The blue ribbon for them is a coveted prize. And while homemade fruit pies are the perfect finale for a family dinner, they've always been considered excellent fare to offer to guests, too — and don't think for a moment that there's not a good bit of competitiveness in the offering of a special pie to dinner guests! Every home pie-maker wants to serve the best pie ever, the perfect fruit pie. But along with this competitiveness goes a remarkable generosity. These recipes are shared, given to whomever wants them. You'll see dozens of them in every community and church cookbook. It would be unthinkable to say, "Sorry, but it's a secret recipe," when asked how to make your pie.

Our native inventiveness has always been put to good use in the making of fruit pies. We add a little nutmeg here, a handful of raisins there, perhaps combine two or more fruits in an unusual way — and then it's our own special pie, unlike any other. But probably the most cherished recipes, though not necessarily the most spectacular, are those that have been handed down in families, sometimes for many generations.

The recipes in this book were all entries in the Stark Bro's Nurseries (Louisiana, Missouri) contest searching for the perfect fruit pie. When the company began its search, no one anticipated how many recipes would be sent in, or what heart-warming comments would accompany them. One woman, for instance, wrote of finding her recipe in the attic of her grandmother's house. Another told of being taught to make a pie 50 years ago by her mother. One wrote that a slice of her pie, reheated in the microwave oven and served with a glass of milk or some vanilla ice cream was a favorite nighttime snack in her family. Still another told how her recipe was an attempt to recapture a delightful time one autumn

INTRODUCTION

at a village restaurant in France. These people shared not only their recipes but a bit of their lives, as well.

It's obvious from many of the pie-makers' comments that the quality of the fruit used is of great importance. One man, for example, said, "The blueberries you use for this recipe should be plump, firm, clean, and deep blue in color. A reddish tinge indicates immaturity; they will not ripen further once picked."

It was a difficult job to narrow down the entries to the award-winners that appear here. All the pies and cobblers submitted had glorious taste, juiciness, and texture. The pies had eye-appeal, too. (Just the sight of a fruit pie is enough to appeal to anyone!) The contestants often made such comments as "the red rhubarb gives this pie a pretty color," or "...sift confectioner's sugar on top for a beautiful effect," or "An authentic feast for eyes and mouth!"

But winners had to be chosen, and here they are. From the approximately 1000 entries received, we have selected over 100 for your enjoyment. In October 1990, Stark Bro's Nurseries awarded the Grand Prize to "Indiana Creamy Peach Pie" (page 62); second and third prizes went to "Blackberry Pinwheels Cobbler" (page 131) and "The Gods' Raspberry Pie" (page 133), respectively. All of these special pies and cobblers are absolutely wonderful, however, and once you begin your own taste-testing, you will want to try them all!

1

Making Perfect
Fruit Pies

CHOOSING AND PREPARING FRUIT

Let's run through the various sorts of fruit — which varieties, particularly of apples, are best for pies, and how to prepare them. Instructions for freezing and canning are included at the end of this chapter, too, since you may well want to capture some of summer's bounty for year-round pie-making.

There are general rules for choosing any fruit: Go by color and a general glow of good health, and beware of any soft, darkened, or caved-in areas or touches of mildew. If you're buying berries in little see-through cartons, turn the boxes over and peer as best you can at the berries on the bottom.

Any fruit pie that does not contain a custard base can be successfully frozen after baking.

APPLES

When you're making an apple pie, you need to use an apple that will hold its shape and not become mush. Certain varieties that are wonderful for other purposes, McIntosh and Gravenstein, for example, tend to become applesauce when cooked. In most pies, you want clearly recognizable pieces or slices of apple. Among the varieties that are especially good for pies are Granny Smith — tart, the favorite of many; Jonathan or Stark Jon-a-Red — somewhat tangy; Golden Delicious — a slightly spicy, sweet flavor; Empire — similar to McIntosh, but holds its shape better; Cortland — an old favorite. Those who use a tart apple such as Granny Smith often add a little more sugar than their pie recipes call for.

If you're buying apples, any available will be ready for use immediately, with no further ripening period. If you grow your own, pick when color and size are at their peak. Do not use apples that feel at all soft.

Unless instructed otherwise, peel the apples and core them. (One easy way to core is to cut the apples vertically into halves or quarters, then scoop out the core and seeds with a paring knife.) Slice or chop, depending on the recipe you're using. If you're peeling and slicing ahead of time, sprinkle the pieces of apple with a little lemon juice to prevent darkening. (This is not necessary if you are using Golden Delicious.)

3

Peaches, Pears, Plums, and Apricots

Like many other fruits, peaches are ready to use when they yield slightly to the touch of your finger. Before you make your delectable peach pie, you will have to skin the peaches and remove their pits. (To peel, plunge the peaches into boiling water for 30 seconds, then put them into cold water immediately. The skins will then pop right off.) If you're not going to use the peaches immediately, sprinkle the cut surfaces with a little lemon juice to prevent darkening.

Pears are picked somewhat green, when the flesh gives just slightly to the touch, then shelf-ripened for five to ten days in a slightly cool, dark place. (Not the refrigerator — the ideal temperature for this ripening is 70°-75° F.) Pears need to be peeled, cored, and cut, then quickly sprinkled with lemon juice to prevent darkening. The old standby pear is the Bartlett, discovered in 1797, but greatly improved since then. Seckel pears, small and spicy, are ready for use when their color changes from yellow-green to light red. The fairly new Asian pears are apple-shaped and a bit more tart than others.

Plums, which come in a remarkable number of colors and sizes, are ripe when they give just a little to finger pressure. They are usually used halved when they're in a pie, although Little Jack Horner seems to have preferred to have them whole. They don't need to be skinned, but the pits do need to be removed.

The apricot has a distinctive flavor, loved by most people. Unless the fruit has been frozen, the skin is tender and does not need to be removed. For most purposes, all you have to do is slit or halve the apricot and remove the pit. ("Freestone" apricots are best to work with.) Apricots are ready to use when they yield slightly to gentle finger-pressure.

Rhubarb

Rhubarb is such a natural for making pies that in parts of the Midwest it used to be known as "pieplant." Nothing could be easier to grow — you'll still find thriving rhubarb patches in the dooryards of long-abandoned houses. It's also available in produce departments in the spring — look for crisp stalks which have not become limp. Red stalks make prettier pies, but green ones taste good, too. To use, rinse the rhubarb and cut it into small pieces. It is cooked before going into pies — and *don't* attempt to use the leaves — they are poisonous!

Rhubarb is often used in conjunction with strawberries, since they taste so good together and they ripen at the same time of year.

CHERRIES AND GRAPES

Cherry pies are the favorite dessert of quite a few people. The only problem with cherries is that they do have to be pitted — a small price to pay since you can buy inexpensive cherry-pitting gadgets that make the job easy. Just rinse the cherries, remove the pits, and they're ready to use. Sour cherries such as Starkspur Montmorency and North Star are the ones generally used for pies, but pies made from sweet cherries have their fans, too.

The best choice for grape pies will always be the seedless varieties. These come in "white," which is actually pale green, in red, or in blue. The skin of seedless grapes is tender enough to eliminate peeling. However, there are those pie-makers partial to such grapes as the famous old Concord that require both deseeding and careful, individual removal of the skins by hand. (New varieties make this removal of skins much easier than it used to be.)

STRAWBERRIES

Have you ever met anyone who didn't like strawberries? Not I! In choosing or picking strawberries, look for color and soundness. If you feel they need washing, make it just a quick rinse.

BLUEBERRIES, BLACKBERRIES, RASPBERRIES, AND THEIR COUSINS

All blueberries make scrumptious pies. Many people have their preferences, though — some for the bigger berries, some for the smaller, which tend to be more tart. Regardless of the size or the variety, the only preparation blueberries need is a careful rinsing and drying and a picking-over to eliminate any hard, small green berries.

Raspberry pies are probably the most symbolic of summer of all pies. Their dark red glow and sweet but tart taste transport you to the summer days of your childhood. As with blueberries, you don't need to do a thing to them before preparing your pie. To tell if they're ready to use in a pie, decide by size and color. This is also true of all the raspberry's relatives

— the blackberry, black raspberry, boysenberry, and elderberry.

FREEZING FRUIT

If you grow your own fruit, you may find yourself with such generous harvests that it's impossible to use all the fruit right away. Even if you depend on store-bought fruit, it is most available, most plentiful, and least costly when it is in season. Either way, it's a great idea to freeze some, so you can make your gorgeous fruit pies all year long.

Berries can be frozen without adding sugar. Some other fruits can be combined with dry sugar before freezing; others do better with a simple sugar syrup (see box for instructions). You'll save yourself some effort at pie-making time if you cut the fruit into whatever size pieces you'll be needing before you freeze it. To use the fruit in a pie, just drain off any sugar syrup or juice.

TWO WAYS TO FREEZE FRUITS IN SUGAR

▼▼▼▼▼▼▼▼▼▼▼▼▼▼▼▼▼▼▼▼▼

SIMPLE SYRUP

Combine 2 cups water with 1¼ to 1½ cups sugar; boil the mixture for 3 or 4 minutes, then cool. Place fruit in freezer container. Pour syrup over fruit, covering it completely. Seal and freeze.

DRY-PACK

Put the sliced fruit in a sealable, plastic freezer bag; add lemon juice or antibrowning agent; shake the bag well; add sugar (½-¾ cup sugar per 1 quart fruit, depending upon sweetness desired); shake again; seal and freeze.

Ascorbic acid or other antibrowning agents. Most fruits (but not berries) will turn brown if not given a little special treatment before freezing. The ideal antibrowning agent is ascorbic acid (vitamin C) in powdered form, mixed with water or syrup (in a ratio of ¼ teaspoon ascorbic acid to each 1 cup water), but other antibrowning agents are also available in most supermarkets and work well. Lemon juice can also be used.

Berries of all sorts *except* strawberries. These are the easiest fruits to freeze. Begin by picking over the fruit. Wash blueberries, but wash other berries only if they are noticeably dirty or pesticide-tainted, then pat dry thoroughly. Put berries into sealable, plastic freezer bags, seal tightly, and place in the freezer. There's nothing to it! For "flash-freezing," spread out the berries on baking sheets, freeze, then pack in sealable, plastic freezer bags. Use the berries, still frozen, exactly as you would if they were fresh.

Cherries. Rinse, pat dry, and pit the cherries, then sprinkle with some ascorbic acid solution or other antibrowning agent. Combine with ½ cup sugar for every 2 cups fruit.

Peaches, nectarines, and apricots. Peaches definitely need to be peeled before freezing; with nectarines and apricots, this is optional. Cut into appropriate-size pieces. All three fruits need to be treated with an ascorbic acid solution or other antibrowning agent and can be packed in a sugar syrup or dry-packed in sugar.

Pears and apples. Pears don't freeze as well as other fruits, and few people feel the need to freeze apples, which store so well. If you want to freeze either fruit, peel and cut into appropriate-size pieces, then quickly use ascorbic acid or another antibrowning agent and pack in a sugar syrup or dry-pack in sugar.

Strawberries. Rinse, dry, trim, and slice (if desired). Then either combine with sugar (¾ cup for each 1 quart berries) or pack in a sugar syrup.

CANNING FRUIT

Since the advent of the home freezer, not as many people "can" their summer fruit. However, for those who lack freezer space or simply prefer home-canned fruit, it's a fairly simple process:

1. Prepare the fruits as you would for freezing, using an antibrowning agent if necessary. Make a light syrup by cooking together 1½ cups sugar and 1 quart water until the sugar is dissolved. (For a heavier syrup, which is more traditional, use 2 cups sugar to 1 quart water. Some home canners even use equal parts of sugar and water.)

2. Pack the fruit in freshly sterilized jars; cover fruit with boiling hot syrup; seal.

3. Process fully submerged in a boiling water bath. For pint jars, process for the following times:

Apples, apricots, grapes, pears, plums — 20 minutes
Cherries, all berries, currants, and rhubarb — 10 minutes
Peaches, nectarines — 25 minutes

If you're using quart jars, add 5 minutes to the processing time for each variety.

Drain the fruit well before using in a pie. (This also applies if you are using commercially canned fruit.)

THE SECRETS OF MAKING GREAT CRUSTS

A pie can't be any better than the crust in which it's encased, so, as good pie-makers have always known, it will be to your advantage to learn how to make great crusts. Fortunately, this is an easy art, once you learn a few tricks. Many of our contestants have included their own special crusts with their recipes, but we also offer some of our own favorites here. No matter how beautiful the filling, a soggy, heavy crust can ruin any pie.

Let's start out with a basic flaky pie crust, then move on to specialized versions like crumb and cookie crusts, as well as toppings.

BASIC FLAKY PIE CRUST

There are two elements that make all the difference: the ingredients you use and the temperature of the ingredients as you work.

Flour. Unbleached white flour will give you the best results, but it does have one flaw — if you plan to refrigerate an unbleached flour dough for a few days before baking, it will turn gray. So, if you wish to use half the dough now and half later on, use "all-purpose" white flour. (If you freeze the dough instead of just refrigerating it, it won't turn gray.) Whole wheat flour, used alone, makes a very heavy crust, but you can, if you wish, substitute it for not more than a quarter of the white flour. Some feel that whole wheat pastry flour, used without any white flour, makes an acceptable crust, but it's sometimes not easy to find. (Try a health food store or food co-op.)

Fats. The possibilities here are butter, margarine, vegetable shortening, and lard; some cooks use oil, though we don't recommend it.

The old standbys are butter and lard, used together in various proportions. This makes a crust that is delicious but not exactly what the doctor ordered for those concerned with cholesterol levels. An all-margarine crust is possible, though it's important to keep the margarine very cold (in fact, you may even wish to start out with it frozen). A good combination is 5 parts cold butter or frozen margarine to 1 part lard or vegetable shortening.

Liquids. Ice water is the usual choice, but any thin, cold liquid can be used. Orange juice, for instance, used half and half with water, makes a lovely crust for certain pies. When you get out the ingredients for your crust, put whatever liquid you're using in a measuring cup along with a few ice cubes. By the time you want to add the liquid, it will be thoroughly cold.

It's impossible to say what the "right amount" of liquid will be, since different flours absorb different amounts of liquid; in addition, the same kind of flour may need more liquid on dry days, less when the humidity is high. If you use too much liquid, you're apt to have a tough crust; too little, and you'll have a crust that falls apart and is difficult to work with. Don't be frightened by these dire predictions, though. The key is to add the liquid slowly and stop when you've added just enough to make the dough hold together nicely.

Salt, Sugar, or Other Seasonings? Use salt if you wish, but it's really unnecessary. Many cooks always add some sugar — a tablespoon or so — to the crust for any fruit pie; others wouldn't dream of doing so. Make your own choice. Other additions are possible. A little grated citrus peel, for instance, can be pleasant, and on occasion you might want to add a few pinches of nutmeg or cinnamon. It's up to you!

Temperature. I have already mentioned the importance of using cold, or even frozen, margarine and of thoroughly chilling whichever liquid you use. This is because it's *vitally* important to keep the fat you're using from becoming soft (or even, heaven forbid, melting) before the crust goes in the oven. This is the true, greatest secret of a flaky crust — the ingredients must be cold, and the crust must be kept chilled as much of the time as possible until it is baked. The alternative is a soggy, heavy crust, which you won't want to acknowledge was made by you.

For this reason, it's important to use *cold* butter or other fat and *ice* water. Also, if you're making crust in a hot kitchen, or if you find it necessary to stop work on the crust, even for a few minutes, pop the dough into your refrigerator until it's cold and firm.

Method. Until fairly recently, all pie crust dough was made by hand, usually by cutting the fat into the flour with a pastry blender or a knife held in each hand. People able to work very quickly even use their fingertips to combine the fat and flour. Using this method, the fat is cut in until the mixture resembles coarse cornmeal, then the liquid is quickly stirred in. Many people still use that method, but most of those who have used a food processor are convinced that it makes the best crust, since the whole process is accomplished so quickly that the dough doesn't have a chance to warm up. The instructions below call for the use of a food processor, but the crust can also be made by hand.

Pie pan. Experts agree that pies made in glass or black steel pie pans have the best, crisp, evenly browned crusts. The worst choice, contrary to what many people think, is a shiny metal pie pan. Most experts grease the inside of the pie pan or spray it with a nonstick vegetable coating.

Rolling out the dough. The two main things to remember when you're rolling out flaky pastry dough are not to kill the dough by over-working it and, as mentioned above, to be sure to keep it cold at all times.

Any sort of rolling pin or other cylindrical shape will do, even a wine or soda bottle in a pinch, but the very best and easiest results come from a fairly large, heavy rolling pin. (The idea is to have the pin do the work, not you.) You can occasionally find a hollow rolling pin, which can be filled with ice water, thus keeping the dough well-chilled while you work.

Place one of your cold little cakes of dough on a lightly floured surface (a bread board, a kitchen counter, a pastry cloth or, especially, a slab of marble, which will stay cool). Some bread boards and pastry cloths come with circles of various sizes printed on them; this can

BASIC PIE CRUST

Yield: 1 double crust or 2 shells for 9-inch pie

▼▼▼▼▼▼▼▼▼▼▼▼▼▼▼▼▼▼▼▼▼▼▼

1¾ CUPS FLOUR
1 TEASPOON SALT (YOU CAN USE LESS OR NONE)
1 TABLESPOON SUGAR (OPTIONAL)
1¼ STICKS COLD BUTTER OR FROZEN MARGARINE
2 TABLESPOONS CHILLED MARGARINE, VEGETABLE SHORTENING, OR LARD
3 TABLESPOONS ICE WATER, IN A MEASURING CUP WITH ICE CUBES

Put the flour (and the salt and sugar, if you're using them) into a food processor fitted with the metal blade. Cut both types of fat into ½-inch pieces and drop into the processor. Process for about 3 seconds, until the flour and fat are barely combined. Remove the ice cubes and pour the ice water into the processor. Process again for 2 or 3 seconds — just until the dough forms a cohesive mass. If the dough doesn't hold together, add a few more drops of very cold water and process briefly again.

Cut the dough in half, shape each half into a flat little cake, wrap well in aluminum foil or plastic wrap and chill for 1-2 hours, or until fully firm. (Will keep for a week refrigerated, and much longer if frozen.)

be quite a help. If the dough is *very* cold and you find it hard to work with, bang it a few times with the rolling pin.

Begin to roll the dough into a circle that is 2 inches larger than your pie pan, rolling from the center outward and not rolling over the edge of the dough. Turning the dough from time to time helps in this process. You may have to sprinkle a little more flour on both the rolling surface and the pin. When you have your circle of dough (and it can be a fairly rough circle), roll it up on your lightly floured rolling pin and unroll it over the pie pan.

Now, ease the dough down into the pan by lifting the edges. Push it down a little around the sides, which you want to be slightly thicker than the bottom. Cut off the excess dough— the best way to do this is to run your rolling pin over the top. Next, push the dough up so it's uniformly about ⅛ inch above the pan.

For a single-crust pie. Do some fluting and/or crimping to make the edge look attractive and to help it adhere to the rim of the pan. This can be done with the back of a fork or by pinching the dough with two fingers of one hand and bringing a finger or knuckle of the other hand up between them.

For a double-crust pie. Don't do anything fancy to the edge quite yet. First, put in your filling, then bring out your second little cake of dough. Roll it, drape it around the rolling pin, and unroll it over the filling. Trim the edges evenly now and crimp or flute them together. Cut slits or little fancy shapes in the top crust to let steam escape. (To be really fancy, cut little leaf or fruit-shaped pieces from the pastry trimmings and attach them with a little cold water to the top crust. Or, for fun, make your slits in the shape of an initial or two.)

Don't let this long list of instructions daunt you. Rolling out pastry dough is a great deal easier and faster than it sounds! After you do it a couple of times, it will be second nature and take just a minute or two.

Blind-baking. Blind-baking means precooking a flaky crust, either completely or partially. For pies containing fillings that do not require baking, this step is obviously necessary.

For pies which will be baked after the filling is added, prebaking of the shell is often skipped, but when it's done, it produces a better crust. (Sometimes the crust threatens to become too brown during the main baking, but aluminum foil placed over the rim of the crust will remedy this.)

For generations, blind-baking has been done by filling the empty pie shell with dry beans or rice. This is to hold the crust down, maintain its shape, and eliminate blistering and shrinkage. This process works well, but it's a bit cumbersome, and leaves you with beans or rice that are unsuitable for any other use. You can also use a double thickness of aluminum foil pressed against the bottom and sides of the pastry before blind-baking. An empty pie pan put on top of the pastry works well, too.

Freezing your pies. All fruit pies, except those made with a custard base, freeze beautifully.

TIMES FOR BLIND-BAKING
▼▼▼▼▼▼▼▼▼▼▼▼▼▼▼▼▼▼▼▼▼

PARTIAL BAKING (BEFORE ADDING A FILLING)

First, prick the shell well with a fork. Line with aluminum foil (see above). Bake at 450° F. until just set — about 10 minutes. Reduce the heat to 375° F., remove the foil, and bake for another 10 minutes, or until the pastry has just begun to take on color. Cool before adding the filling.

COMPLETELY BAKED PIE SHELL

Follow the above instructions, but cook just a little longer, until the edges of the crust are tan.

When you're making one pie, it's very little effort to make several at a time, serving one now and freezing the rest for future use.

The main questions are whether to freeze the pies before or after baking, and if you freeze them before baking, whether or not to thaw them before baking. We suggest freezing before the pies are baked and baking them directly from the freezer until the crust is golden brown (about 45 minutes at 425° F.).

If it seems more convenient to bake your pie before freezing, then thaw before rewarming. The crust will not be of such high quality, and the pie will not seem as fresh, but you'll still have a very good pie.

A wily method you might want to try is to prepare a fruit filling, put it in a sealable plastic freezer bag or aluminum foil pouch, place in a pie pan, and freeze. When you want a pie, simply remove the bag or foil and place the pie-shaped frozen filling in a crust.

HEALTHY FRUIT PIES

As we have become increasingly aware of how important the food we eat is to our health and general sense of well-being, many of us have attempted to cut back on our sugar and fat intake. Several of the recipe contestants made special note of the fact that in developing their recipes, they were making a conscious effort to provide healthier desserts for themselves and their families. Beginning with ingredients as naturally sweet and nutritious as fruits makes it relatively simple to create desserts that are as tempting and delectable as they are good for you. For recipes of special interest to those seeking healthy alternatives to too-rich final courses, see especially the following:

CRUMB CRUST

Everyone is familiar with the graham cracker crumb crusts used for many cheese pies and cheese cakes, but many people have never made a pie with a crust made from cookie crumbs. They've missed a lot — a ginger snap crust, for instance, is a real winner, as is one made from the inimitable and beloved Oreos, Hydrox, or other sandwich cookies. You'll find a number of good crumb crusts in the award-winning recipes in this book, but here is a simple one that can be made in many different flavors.

▼▼▼▼▼▼▼▼▼▼▼▼▼▼▼▼▼▼▼▼▼

1½ CUPS CRUMBS FROM GRAHAM CRACKERS, GINGER SNAPS, CHOCOLATE WAFERS,
CHOCOLATE SANDWICH COOKIES, ZWIEBACK, ETC.
1 TABLESPOON SUGAR OR HONEY (OPTIONAL)
4 TABLESPOONS MELTED BUTTER OR MARGARINE
½ CUP CHOPPED NUTS *AND/OR* ½ TEASPOON CINNAMON (OPTIONAL)

Combine all the ingredients and, using your fingers, spread in a 9-inch pie pan or a springform pan. Press firmly. If you're using a filling that must be baked in the pie shell, your crust is ready to use now. Simply chill the crust while you prepare the filling. If the filling doesn't require baking, put the crumb crust in a 350° F. oven for 10 minutes. Cool thoroughly before adding the filling.

COOKIE CRUST

This crust is made from a dough very similar to cookie dough. It makes a nice, firm base for a pie — also, no one expects it to be "flaky," and it doesn't need to be rolled.

▼▼▼▼▼▼▼▼▼▼▼▼▼▼▼▼▼▼▼▼▼▼

¼ CUP SUGAR OR TO TASTE
½ CUP SOFTENED BUTTER OR MARGARINE
½ TEASPOON PURE VANILLA EXTRACT
1 CUP FLOUR

Beat the sugar and butter together until well creamed. Add first the vanilla, then the flour. Place in a pie pan or springform pan and press into the sides and bottom, using your fingers.

You can add your own touches—a little grated orange peel, a touch of nutmeg—whatever sounds good and would complement the pie's filling.

CRUMB, STREUSEL, AND OATMEAL TOPPINGS

Crumb or streusel toppings add a nice crunch and a bit of extra flavor, and better still, they're a great deal easier to make and use than the usual top crust of flaky pastry. The simplest and one of the best crumb toppings is made by reserving ¼ to ½ cup of the crumb mixture you're using for the crust to sprinkle on top of the pie. This, however, is more of a garnish than a top crust; a true crumb or streusel topping is more like the following.

▼▼▼▼▼▼▼▼▼▼▼▼▼▼▼▼▼▼▼▼▼▼

¾ CUP FLOUR
½ TEASPOON CINNAMON
¼ TEASPOON NUTMEG
½ CUP BROWN SUGAR
4 TABLESPOONS BUTTER OR MARGARINE

Combine the flour with the cinnamon, nutmeg, and brown sugar. Cut in the butter or margarine with a pastry blender or your fingertips until the topping resembles coarse bread crumbs. Sprinkle the mixture over the top of a pie before baking.

OATMEAL TOPPING

Follow the instructions for the above streusel topping, adding ½ cup oatmeal and using *only* ½ cup flour.

2

Perfect Fruit Pie Recipes

Apple Pies

▼▼▼

STARK-RAVING GRAND
Yield: 6-8 servings

Part of my family since before the Revolutionary War, this recipe came from England to New England with my great-great-whatever grandmother. The original directions called for greening apples. When I was younger, the pie was baked in a woodstove in huge pans. It was meant to stand for a day and then covered with a "puff or tart paste."

▼▼▼▼▼▼▼▼▼▼▼▼▼▼▼▼▼▼▼▼▼

2 TABLESPOONS BROWN SUGAR
2 TEASPOONS GRATED LEMON PEEL
2 TEASPOONS GRATED OR GROUND GINGER
1 TEASPOON CINNAMON
½ TEASPOON MACE
¼ TEASPOON GROUND CLOVES
PASTRY FOR TWO 9-INCH PIE CRUSTS
2-4 TABLESPOONS LEMON OR ORANGE MARMALADE
2 POUNDS STARKSPUR RED ROME BEAUTY APPLES, OR OTHER BAKING APPLES

Preheat oven to 425° F. Mix together brown sugar, lemon peel, and spices. Put into a pastry-lined 9-inch pie pan half of the sugar mixture. Dribble 1½-2 tablespoons marmalade over it.

Pare, quarter, and core apples and cut them into thin bits (about 6 cups). Put half of the apples into crust. Sprinkle with remaining sugar mixture. Dribble another 1-2 tablespoons marmalade over it. Add remaining apples.

Roll out remaining pastry slightly larger than pie pan, wet rim of pan, and fit pastry on top of pie. Press edges all around with a fork. Make a small hole in the middle of the pastry with the point of a knife. Bake for 40 minutes, or until apples are tender.

Jacqueline B. Jones, Cheney, WA

YUMMY APPLE-Y PIE

Yield: 8 servings

▼▼▼▼▼▼▼▼▼▼▼▼▼▼▼▼▼▼▼▼▼▼

1 CUP SUGAR

2 TABLESPOONS ALL-PURPOSE FLOUR

1 CUP ORANGE JUICE

1 TEASPOON NUTMEG

4 TABLESPOONS BUTTER

4 LARGE APPLES, CHOPPED

½ CUP RAISINS

TWO 9-INCH PIE SHELLS, UNBAKED

Preheat oven to 450° F. Heat sugar, flour, juice, nutmeg, and butter until butter melts. Pour over apples and raisins in pie shell. Put on lattice top crust. Bake for 10 minutes. Reduce heat to 350° F. and bake for 20 minutes more.

Nellie Butler, Bruceton, TN

"I-SPY" PIE

Yield: 8 servings

▼▼▼▼▼▼▼▼▼▼▼▼▼▼▼▼▼▼▼▼▼

PASTRY FOR TWO 10-INCH PIE CRUSTS
5 CUPS UNPEELED, CORED, AND SLICED APPLES
¾ CUP SUGAR
3 TABLESPOONS AMARETTO LIQUEUR
1 TABLESPOON LEMON JUICE
PINCH SALT
¼ TEASPOON CINNAMON
DASH NUTMEG
2 TABLESPOONS ALL-PURPOSE FLOUR
6 TEASPOONS BUTTER

Preheat oven to 400° F. Place bottom crust in a 10-inch pie plate. Fill with apples. Add sugar, liqueur, lemon juice, salt, cinnamon, and nutmeg. Shake flour over apples and dot with butter. Cover with top crust. Seal and flute edge. Prick or slit top crust. Bake for 15 minutes. Reduce heat to 350° F. and bake for 45-50 minutes more, or until apples are tender and crust is golden brown.

Anne Wamsley, Eaton Rapids, MI

"DELICIOUS" APPLE PIE

Yield: 6 servings

My mother, Mrs. John E. Shannon, won first place in an apple pie contest many years ago— before I was born in 1918. I grew up on a farm in the Hickory Grove neighborhood near the Stark Bro's Nursery and always thought it was a treat to ride my pony up to see Theodasia and Paul Jr. at the orchard.

▼▼▼▼▼▼▼▼▼▼▼▼▼▼▼▼▼▼▼▼▼

¼ CUP ALL-PURPOSE FLOUR

¼ CUP SUGAR (MORE, IF APPLES ARE TART)

½ TEASPOON CINNAMON

¼ TEASPOON ALLSPICE

¼ TEASPOON NUTMEG

ONE 9-INCH PIE SHELL, UNBAKED

4-5 MEDIUM-SIZE GOLDEN DELICIOUS APPLES

2 TABLESPOONS LOW-CALORIE MARGARINE

¼ CUP WARM WATER

CINNAMON

Preheat oven to 350° F. Mix together flour, sugar, cinnamon, allspice, and nutmeg. Place flour mixture into pie shell. Slice apples into pie shell. Dot apples with margarine. Pour warm water over apples. Sprinkle with small amount of cinnamon. Cover with a lid or aluminum foil and bake for about 45 minutes. Remove foil or lid approximately 15 minutes before pie is done. There is no top crust.

Frances Shannon Shaw, Alexandria, LA

HOOSIER DEEP-DISH APPLE PIE

Yield: 8 servings

▼▼▼▼▼▼▼▼▼▼▼▼▼▼▼▼▼▼▼▼▼▼

CRUST:

3 CUPS ALL-PURPOSE FLOUR
3 TABLESPOONS SUGAR
½ CUP BUTTER
ONE 8-OUNCE CONTAINER SOUR CREAM

FILLING:

8 LARGE ROME BEAUTY APPLES
(APPROXIMATELY 3½ POUNDS)
1 CUP SUGAR
4 TABLESPOONS ALL-PURPOSE FLOUR
1 TABLESPOON FRESH LEMON JUICE
2 TEASPOONS GRATED LEMON PEEL
½ TEASPOON CINNAMON
¼ TEASPOON NUTMEG
1 EGG YOLK, BEATEN

Preheat oven to 350° F.

For crust, combine flour and sugar. Cut in butter with pastry blender. Stir in sour cream. Refrigerate at least 1 hour.

For filling, peel, core, and slice apples. In a large bowl, combine apples, sugar, flour, lemon juice, lemon peel, and spices.

On a lightly floured surface, roll out half the dough to a 13-inch circle. Fit into a 9-inch pie pan, leaving a 1-inch overhang. Put apple mixture into crust. Roll out remaining dough and fit over apples. Flute edges. Cut vents in top crust and brush with egg yolk. Bake for 50 minutes.

Jackie Cannon, Evansville, IL

HONEYAPPLE PIE

Yield: 6 servings

In 1984, this pie won first place in a local cooking contest. I baked it in a wood burning cookstove, using hickory to get the temperature up quickly and oak to bake the pie.

▼▼▼▼▼▼▼▼▼▼▼▼▼▼▼▼▼▼▼▼▼▼▼

2 CUPS SIFTED ALL-PURPOSE FLOUR
¼ CUP WHEAT GERM
1 TEASPOON SALT
⅔ CUP BUTTER-FLAVORED SHORTENING
½ CUP ICE WATER
3 CUPS PEELED AND SLICED STARKSPUR GOLDEN DELICIOUS APPLES
3 CUPS PEELED AND SLICED JON-A-RED APPLES

½ CUP RAISINS
2 TABLESPOONS ALL-PURPOSE FLOUR
DASH SALT
½ CUP HONEY
1 TABLESPOON BUTTER
1 TABLESPOON LEMON JUICE
½ TEASPOON CINNAMON

For crust, sift 2 cups flour, wheat germ, and salt together. Cut in shortening. Gradually sprinkle ice water over flour mixture, and stir until the particles are uniformly moistened and just stick together. Divide into two balls—one slightly larger than the other. Roll out larger piece of dough and line a 9-inch pie plate. Roll out other dough and set aside.

Preheat oven to 450° F. Mix apples and raisins together. Blend 2 tablespoons flour, dash of salt, and honey. Spread one-quarter of the flour mixture over bottom pie crust. Stir remaining flour mixture into apples. Pour into pie crust, dot with butter, and sprinkle with lemon juice and cinnamon. Moisten edge of pastry, lay top crust over apples, and press down gently around edge to seal. Trim pastry to ½ inch beyond rim; turn overhang under lower pastry so fold is even with plate rim. Press down gently all around edge and flute with finger. Cut air vents in top of crust. Bake for 15 minutes. Reduce heat to 325° F. and bake for 35 minutes more, or until juice is bubbly and crust is nicely browned.

Maureen Patricia Darby, Lebanon, MO

MY PERFECT APPLE PIE

Yield: 6 servings

▼▼▼▼▼▼▼▼▼▼▼▼▼▼▼▼▼▼▼▼▼▼

1 TABLESPOON LEMON JUICE (OPTIONAL)
1 CUP SUGAR
2 TABLESPOONS ALL-PURPOSE FLOUR
1 TEASPOON CINNAMON
⅛ TEASPOON NUTMEG
⅛ TEASPOON SALT
6-8 TART APPLES, PEELED, CORED, AND THINLY SLICED (APPROXIMATELY **6** CUPS)
PASTRY FOR TWO **9**-INCH DEEP-DISH PIE CRUSTS
2 TABLESPOONS BUTTER
SUGAR

Preheat oven to 400° F. If apples lack tartness, sprinkle with 1 tablespoon lemon juice. Combine sugar, flour, cinnamon, nutmeg, and salt. Mix with apples. Line a 9-inch pie pan with pastry. Fill with apple mixture and dot with butter. Put on top crust, cutting slits for steam to escape. Seal edges. Sprinkle with sugar. Bake for 50 minutes. Serve warm or cool.

George N. Melson, Mexico, MO

SUGAR-FREE APPLE PIE

Yield: 6-8 servings

Apple juice may be used as a sweetener in fruit pies other than apple, with little effect on the predominate fruit's flavor. If it's important that you use absolutely no sugar, check the label on the concentrate to be sure sugar isn't listed as an ingredient; some concentrates labeled "natural" do contain sugar.

▼▼▼▼▼▼▼▼▼▼▼▼▼▼▼▼▼▼▼▼▼

2⅔ CUPS ALL-PURPOSE FLOUR

2 STICKS BUTTER OR MARGARINE, AT ROOM TEMPERATURE

5 TABLESPOONS ICE WATER

12 MEDIUM RED APPLES

4 OUNCES FROZEN, UNSWEETENED APPLE JUICE CONCENTRATE, UNDILUTED

2-3 TABLESPOONS CORNSTARCH

1 TEASPOON NUTMEG

2 TABLESPOONS MELTED BUTTER OR MARGARINE

HEAVY CREAM

Preheat oven to 375° F.

For crust, mix flour and margarine. Add ice water. Mix until dough forms. Do not overmix. Place in freezer for 10 minutes. Roll out for a two-crust pie. (This can be made in two halves for ease.)

For filling, peel and slice apples. Use more or less apples, if desired. Mix frozen apple juice concentrate, cornstarch, and nutmeg with apples, and place mixture in bottom crust. Spread half the melted butter or margarine over apples. Cover with top crust, seal crust, and spread remaining butter or margarine on the crust. Bake for 50 minutes or until bubbly, plus 5 minutes. Top with homemade, unsweetened whipped cream.

K.M. Westbrook, Webberville, MI

GOLDEN DELICIOUS APPLE-WALNUT UPSIDE-DOWN PIE

Yield: 8-10 servings

▼▼▼▼▼▼▼▼▼▼▼▼▼▼▼▼▼▼▼▼▼▼

5 TABLESPOONS MELTED BUTTER OR MARGARINE
½ CUP BROWN SUGAR
½ CUP CHOPPED BLACK WALNUTS
PASTRY FOR TWO 10-INCH PIE CRUSTS
4 CUPS THICKLY SLICED APPLES (¾-INCH PIECES)
1⅛ CUPS GRANULATED SUGAR
4 TABLESPOONS ALL-PURPOSE FLOUR
¾ TABLESPOON CINNAMON
⅛ TEASPOON NUTMEG
¼ TEASPOON SALT

Preheat oven to 375° F. Combine butter and brown sugar and spread in bottom of a 10-inch pie pan. Sprinkle walnuts over butter. Roll dough ½-inch thick. Line over nuts, being careful not to break crust. Trim crust evenly with pan. Fill with apples.

Combine granulated sugar, flour, cinnamon, nutmeg, and salt. Sprinkle over apples. Put on top crust. Trim and seal. Roll edges toward center. (There should be no crust touching pie pan rim.) Bake for 55 minutes. Run knife around edge of pan to loosen pie. Turn upside down on a plate. Let stand 2 minutes and remove pan.

Elsie I. Cook, Loveland, OH

SOUR CREAM APPLE PIE

Yield: 6 servings

▼▼▼▼▼▼▼▼▼▼▼▼▼▼▼▼▼▼▼▼▼▼

½ CUP SUGAR

1 TABLESPOON ALL-PURPOSE FLOUR

¼ TEASPOON CINNAMON

¼ TEASPOON NUTMEG

6 CUPS PEELED, CORED, AND SLICED TART APPLES

ONE 9-INCH PIE SHELL, UNBAKED

1 CUP SOUR CREAM

¼ CUP BROWN SUGAR

NUTMEG

Preheat oven to 400° F. Combine sugar, flour, cinnamon, and nutmeg. Stir into apples. Arrange in pie shell. Cover loosely with aluminum foil. Bake for 50-55 minutes, or until apples are tender. Remove foil. Combine sour cream and brown sugar. Pour evenly over apples. Sprinkle lightly with nutmeg. Bake for 2-3 minutes more, or just until sour cream topping is set.

Laura Cox, Abilene, KS

CIDER APPLE PIE
Yield: 8 servings

▼▼▼▼▼▼▼▼▼▼▼▼▼▼▼▼▼▼▼▼▼▼▼

PASTRY FOR ONE 9-INCH PIE CRUST
4-5 BAKING APPLES
1 TABLESPOON LEMON JUICE
½ CUP SUGAR
3 EGGS
1 CUP HEAVY CREAM
¼ CUP APPLE CIDER
¼ TEASPOON NUTMEG
2 TABLESPOONS SUGAR

Preheat oven to 400° F. Prepare pie crust and flute edges.

Peel, quarter, core, and cut apples into ⅛-inch slices. Toss apple slices with lemon juice and ½-cup sugar in a large bowl. Arrange, rounded side down, starting at the outside edge of pie crust, in two circles in bottom of crust.

Bake at 400° F. for 10 minutes. Reduce heat to 350° F., and continue baking for 20 minutes.

Beat eggs slightly in a medium-sized bowl. Stir in cream, apple cider, and nutmeg. Pour over apples. Continue baking for 15 minutes more. Sprinkle with 2 tablespoons sugar. Bake for 15 minutes more, or until top is golden. Cool for 2 hours before cutting.

Michaela Walsh, Auburn, WA

APPLE STREUSEL

Yield: 24 servings

▼▼▼▼▼▼▼▼▼▼▼▼▼▼▼▼▼▼▼▼▼

4 CUPS ALL-PURPOSE FLOUR
1 TEASPOON SALT
2 TEASPOONS BAKING POWDER
1 CUP BUTTER OR MARGARINE
2 CUPS SUGAR
2 EGGS, SLIGHTLY BEATEN
1 QUART HOMEMADE APPLESAUCE
1 TEASPOON CINNAMON
¼ CUP WHEAT GERM, OR ¼ CUP FINELY CHOPPED WALNUTS
BUTTER

Preheat oven to 350° F. Sift together flour, salt, and baking powder. Cut in butter. Add sugar and cut again. Add eggs. Blend together with forks. Pat three-quarters of the flour mixture onto a 10" x 15" x 1" ungreased jelly roll pan.

Cover crust with applesauce and sprinkle with cinnamon. Add wheat germ or nuts to remaining flour mixture, then sprinkle flour mixture on top of applesauce. Dot with additional butter. Bake for 1 hour or until golden brown.

Mary Calliea, Port Sanilac, MI

MICROWAVE APPLE STREUSEL PIE

Yield: 6 servings

▼▼▼▼▼▼▼▼▼▼▼▼▼▼▼▼▼▼▼▼▼▼

FILLING:

¾-1 CUP BROWN SUGAR

¼ CUP ALL-PURPOSE FLOUR

1 TEASPOON CINNAMON

½ TEASPOON NUTMEG

DASH OF SALT

4 CUPS PEELED AND SLICED JON-A-RED APPLES

2 TABLESPOONS LEMON JUICE

2 TABLESPOONS BUTTER

ONE 9-INCH PIE SHELL, BAKED IN A MICROWAVE-SAFE DISH

TOPPING:

½ CUP ALL-PURPOSE FLOUR OR ROLLED OATS

¼ CUP BROWN SUGAR

2 TABLESPOONS BUTTER AT ROOM TEMPERATURE

½ TEASPOON CINNAMON

¼ CUP CHOPPED NUTS

¼ CUP SHREDDED COCONUT

For filling, mix together sugar, flour, cinnamon, nutmeg, and salt. Add apples. Toss until well coated. Sprinkle with lemon juice. Place in cooled pie shell. Dot with butter.

For topping, mix together all the topping ingredients until crumbly. Sprinkle over apples. Microwave on HIGH (100 percent) for 10-12 minutes, or until apples are tender.

Cathy Dyer, Cookeville, TN

THE BEST APPLE PIE EVER

Yield: 8 servings

▼▼▼▼▼▼▼▼▼▼▼▼▼▼▼▼▼▼▼▼▼

CRUST:
1½ CUPS ALL-PURPOSE FLOUR
¼ CUP GRANULATED SUGAR
½ TEASPOON SALT
1 TEASPOON CINNAMON
½ CUP PLUS 2 TABLESPOONS BUTTER OR
MARGARINE
¼ CUP CIDER OR APPLE JUICE

FILLING:
8 McINTOSH APPLES, PEELED, CORED, AND
SLICED
1⅔ CUPS SOUR CREAM

⅓ CUP ALL-PURPOSE FLOUR
½ TEASPOON SALT
1 EGG, SLIGHTLY BEATEN
2 TEASPOONS VANILLA EXTRACT

TOPPING:
1 CUP CHOPPED WALNUTS
½ CUP ALL-PURPOSE FLOUR
⅓ CUP BROWN SUGAR
½ CUP BUTTER OR MARGARINE, AT ROOM
TEMPERATURE
⅓ CUP GRANULATED SUGAR
1 TABLESPOON CINNAMON

Preheat oven to 450° F.

For crust, mix all dry ingredients together and cut in butter until crumbly. Add cider and mix until moistened. Roll to fit a 10-inch quiche pan, keeping sides high.

For filling, mix all filling ingredients together. Pour into pie crust. Put aluminum foil on edge of crust so it will not burn. Bake for 10 minutes. Reduce heat to 350° F. and continue baking for 40 minutes more.

For topping, mix all topping ingredients together and sprinkle over top of pie. Bake for 15 minutes at 350° F.

Kay Crockett, Springdale, OH

LAURA'S DUTCH APPLE PIE
Yield: 8 servings

▼▼▼▼▼▼▼▼▼▼▼▼▼▼▼▼▼▼▼▼▼

PASTRY FOR ONE 9-INCH OR 10-INCH PIE CRUST

FILLING:
6 CUPS PEELED AND SLICED APPLES
½ CUP GRANULATED SUGAR
½ CUP FIRMLY PACKED BROWN SUGAR
1 TEASPOON CINNAMON
¼ TEASPOON NUTMEG
½ TEASPOON GROUND CLOVES

TOPPING:
¾ CUP ALL-PURPOSE FLOUR
½ CUP FIRMLY PACKED BROWN SUGAR
1 TEASPOON CINNAMON
¼ TEASPOON NUTMEG
¼ TEASPOON GROUND CLOVES
½ CUP BUTTER

Preheat oven to 425° F. Line 9- or 10-inch pie pan with pastry.
Mix together filling ingredients and place in pastry-lined pan.
Mix together all topping ingredients with your fingers to make a soft, crumbly mixture. Sprinkle topping mixture on top of apple mixture and bake for 45 minutes. Serve topped with whipped cream or ice cream, if desired.

Laura Baldwin, West Fort Ann, NY

DUTCH APPLE PIE

Yield: 6 servings

▼▼▼▼▼▼▼▼▼▼▼▼▼▼▼▼▼▼▼▼

CRUMBS:

2 CUPS ALL-PURPOSE FLOUR
1 CUP BROWN SUGAR
½ CUP QUICK OATS
1 TEASPOON SALT
¾ CUP MELTED BUTTER

FILLING:

1¼ CUPS WATER
⅔ CUP GRANULATED SUGAR
3 TABLESPOONS CORNSTARCH
¼ TEASPOON SALT
1 TEASPOON VANILLA EXTRACT
2 CUPS DICED APPLES

Preheat oven to 350° F.

For crumbs, mix together all crumb ingredients. Reserve 1 cup crumbs for topping. Pat remaining crumbs into a 9-inch pie pan for the crust.

For filling, bring water and granulated sugar to a boil. Slowly add cornstarch, salt, and vanilla. Cook for 1 minute. When thick, remove from heat and add apples. Pour into crust and top with reserved crumbs. Bake for 40-45 minutes, or until crust is nicely browned. (A 9-inch, unbaked pie shell can also be used instead of the crumb mixture.)

Mrs. Erma Yutzy, Drakesville, IO

GRANNY'S HAND PIE

Yield: 12 servings

This is an old family recipe from my mother, who came to this country in 1909 from Hungary at the age of 17. The grandchildren were very fond of our granny's pie since it could be picked up and eaten; hence, they called it "Granny's Hand Pie." It was their favorite after-school treat.

▼▼▼▼▼▼▼▼▼▼▼▼▼▼▼▼▼▼▼▼▼▼

2½ CUPS ALL-PURPOSE FLOUR
½ TEASPOON SALT
½ TEASPOON BAKING POWDER
⅔ CUP WELL-CHILLED VEGETABLE
SHORTENING
1 EGG YOLK
ICE WATER
¾ CUP SUGAR

1 TEASPOON CINNAMON
6 GRANNY SMITH APPLES, PEELED AND
THINLY SLICED
2 OUNCES CHOPPED NUTS (OPTIONAL)
½ CUP GOLDEN RAISINS
BUTTER
CONFECTIONERS' SUGAR

Preheat oven to 375° F.

Combine first three ingredients. Cut in shortening to make crumbs the size of small peas. Beat egg yolk in measuring cup. Add enough ice water to make ⅓ cup and add to flour mixture. Work to form a ball. Divide dough in half and roll to fit bottom and up the sides of a 9" x 13" pan which has been slightly greased.

Combine sugar and cinnamon and stir into apples with the nuts and raisins. Dot with butter. Roll out remaining dough and place over apples, which have been spooned over bottom dough. Seal edges well and make slits in top. Bake for 50 minutes or until golden. When cool, sprinkle with confectioners' sugar and cut into 3-inch squares.

Louise Cinciripini, Waterloo, IL

FRIED APPLE PIES

Yield: 4-6 servings

From my mom, who made these when I was a kid back in the 1940s.

▼▼▼▼▼▼▼▼▼▼▼▼▼▼▼▼▼▼▼▼▼

5 CUPS DRIED JONATHAN APPLES
WATER
4 CUPS SUGAR
1 TEASPOON CINNAMON
PASTRY FOR TWO 9-INCH PIE CRUSTS

Combine apples with enough water to cover. Cook for about 15-20 minutes or until tender. Mash apples with a potato masher. Add sugar and cinnamon and let cool. Cut pastry dough into 5" x 8" pieces and place ½ cup apple mixture in each piece. Fold over and pinch edges of crust together. Fry until browned in a well-greased, iron skillet.

Mrs. June Leap, Mack's Creek, MO

COUNTRY DUMPLINGS

Yield: 8 servings

▼▼▼▼▼▼▼▼▼▼▼▼▼▼▼▼▼▼▼▼▼▼

SYRUP:
1 CUP SUGAR
3 TABLESPOONS BUTTER
2 CUPS WATER
⅓ TEASPOON CINNAMON

SAUCE:
⅓ CUP SUGAR
2 TABLESPOONS CORNSTARCH
¼ TEASPOON SALT
2 CUPS WATER

¼ CUP BUTTER
2 TEASPOONS VANILLA EXTRACT
DASH NUTMEG

FILLING:
PASTRY FOR ONE 9-INCH PIE CRUST
3-4 CUPS CHOPPED APPLES
8 TABLESPOONS SUGAR
CINNAMON
NUTMEG
8 DOTS BUTTER

Preheat oven to 425° F.

For syrup, mix all ingredients in a saucepan on medium heat.

For sauce, stir all ingredients together in a saucepan on medium heat until thick.

For filling, divide pastry dough into eight parts. Take each ball of dough and roll it out on a floured surface. Place ½ cup apples in the center of each rolled portion with 1 tablespoon sugar, dash of cinnamon and nutmeg, and a dot of butter. Pull dough around apples and place in a 11" x 8" x 2" baking pan. Pour the hot syrup around dumplings. Bake for 15 minutes. Reduce heat to 350° F. and continue baking for 40 minutes more. Serve with Sauce and ice cream.

Joy Smith, Clifftop, WV

OVEN-FRESH APPLE TURNOVERS

Yield: 6 servings

▼▼▼▼▼▼▼▼▼▼▼▼▼▼▼▼▼▼▼▼▼▼

1½ CUPS ALL-PURPOSE FLOUR
½ TEASPOON SALT
½ CUP VEGETABLE SHORTENING
½ CUP WATER
6 FRESH APPLES, PEELED AND THINLY SLICED
CINNAMON, OR OTHER SPICE YOU PREFER
SUGAR, IF DESIRED

Preheat oven to 400° F. Mix together well flour, salt, and shortening. Add water and work into a ball. Do not overwork. Divide into six balls. Roll each ball thinly. Place apple slices with spice and sugar on half of circle. Fold over, leaving enough of bottom to fold up and over edge to seal. Bake for about 45-60 minutes or until golden brown.

Mrs. John B. Duncan, Maceo, KY

FRESH APPLE SQUARES

Yield: 6-8 servings

▼▼▼▼▼▼▼▼▼▼▼▼▼▼▼▼▼▼▼▼▼

CRUST:

1½ CUPS WHOLE WHEAT PASTRY FLOUR

1½ TEASPOONS SUGAR

½ TEASPOON SALT

⅓ CUP SAFFLOWER OIL

¼ CUP SKIM MILK

FILLING:

¼ CUP SUGAR

1½ TEASPOONS CINNAMON

⅛ TEASPOON SALT, OR LESS

2 TABLESPOONS WHOLE WHEAT PASTRY FLOUR

6 CUPS PEELED, CORED, QUARTERED, AND SLICED ROME APPLES

Preheat oven to 375° F.

For crust, in a large bowl, mix together dry crust ingredients. In a small bowl, mix together wet crust ingredients. Mix wet ingredients into dry and combine well, using hands. Press two-thirds of mixture in the bottom of a 7" x 11" baking pan, reserving remaining dough to crumble on top.

For filling, combine dry ingredients and toss with apples. Pour over crust and crumble reserved dough on top.

Bake for 50-60 minutes, covered with aluminum foil. Remove foil for the last 10 minutes. Let cool at least 30 minutes before cutting into squares to serve. May garnish with a dollop of nonfat vanilla yogurt.

M.J. Helkenn, Detroit, MI

SNOWY FROSTED APPLE SQUARES

Yield: 24 servings

If the apples are sweet, this recipe may be made without the sugar.

▼▼▼▼▼▼▼▼▼▼▼▼▼▼▼▼▼▼▼▼▼▼

1 CUP VEGETABLE SHORTENING
(OR ½ CUP SHORTENING AND ½ CUP MARGARINE)
2¼ CUPS ALL-PURPOSE FLOUR
½ TEASPOON SALT
MILK
2 EGGS, SEPARATED
1½ CUPS CORNFLAKES
5 CUPS SLICED APPLES
1 CUP SUGAR
1½ TEASPOONS CINNAMON

GLAZE:
1¼ CUPS CONFECTIONERS' SUGAR
3 TABLESPOONS WATER
½ TEASPOON VANILLA EXTRACT

Preheat oven to 350° F.

Cut shortening into flour and salt. Add enough milk to beaten egg yolks to make ⅔ cup liquid. Add to flour mixture and toss lightly with a fork to moisten. Divide dough and roll larger half to fit a 15½" x 10½" jelly roll pan.

Sprinkle on cornflakes, apples, sugar, and cinnamon. Top with other half of crust. Beat egg whites until frothy, and spread over top. Bake for 50 minutes.

For glaze, mix together confectioners' sugar, water, and vanilla. Pour glaze over squares while still warm.

Elvarie Ihnen, Golden, IL

APPLE-RAISIN CRISP

Yield: 4-6 servings

▼▼▼▼▼▼▼▼▼▼▼▼▼▼▼▼▼▼▼▼▼▼

4 CUPS SLICED APPLES
½ CUP RAISINS
1 TABLESPOON LEMON JUICE
⅓ CUP ROLLED OATS
½ CUP BROWN SUGAR
½ CUP CHOPPED WALNUTS
½ TEASPOON SALT
1 TABLESPOON CINNAMON
⅓ CUP MELTED BUTTER

Preheat oven to 350° F. Grease a 1½-quart shallow baking dish. Place apples, raisins, and lemon juice in baking dish. Combine all dry ingredients in a small bowl. Add butter and mix until crumbly. Sprinkle over apples and bake for 30 minutes.

Nick Marrazzo, Morrisville, PA

APPLE CRISP

Yield: 6-8 servings

▼▼▼▼▼▼▼▼▼▼▼▼▼▼▼▼▼▼▼▼▼

5 CUPS PEELED AND SLICED BAKING APPLES
1 CUP BROWN SUGAR
1 CUP SIFTED ALL-PURPOSE FLOUR
¾ CUP ROLLED OATS
1 TEASPOON CINNAMON
½ TEASPOON MACE
½ CUP MELTED BUTTER OR MARGARINE

Preheat oven to 350° F. Place apples in a greased 2-quart baking dish. Blend remaining ingredients until crumbly. Spread this mixture over apples. Bake for 30 minutes, or until tender and topping is golden brown. Serve with cream or ice cream.

Mrs. Mary Lee Peery, Kingsport, TN

APPLE CRACKLE

Yield: 6-8 servings

▼▼▼▼▼▼▼▼▼▼▼▼▼▼▼▼▼▼▼▼▼

Filling:

5 CUPS UNPEELED AND SLICED APPLES
½-¾ CUP GRANULATED SUGAR
2 TABLESPOONS ALL-PURPOSE FLOUR
⅓ CUP MELTED BUTTER

Topping:

⅓ CUP ALL-PURPOSE FLOUR
½ CUP ROLLED OATS
½ CUP BROWN SUGAR
PINCH SALT

Preheat oven to 350° F.

For filling, place half of the apples in a greased 1½-quart baking dish. Then half of the sugar and flour should be sprinkled over apples. Place remaining apples on top and sprinkle with remaining sugar and flour.

For topping, mix all ingredients. Sprinkle over top of apples and press down. Pour melted butter over apples and topping. Bake for approximately 45-60 minutes.

Janet R. Shelton, Palmyra, VA

EASY APPLE CHEESE PIE
Yield: 6 servings

▼▼▼▼▼▼▼▼▼▼▼▼▼▼▼▼▼▼▼▼▼

1 CUP SUGAR
1 CUP ALL-PURPOSE FLOUR
1 STICK MARGARINE, AT ROOM TEMPERATURE
4-5 LARGE APPLES, SLICED
1 CUP GRATED CHEDDAR CHEESE
⅓ CUP HOT WATER

Preheat oven to 350° F.

Mix sugar, flour, and margarine until it is mealy. Press half of the flour mixture in the bottom of a deep-dish baking pan. Place apples on top of flour mixture, alternating with cheese. Sprinkle the remaining flour mixture over the top of apples. Punch holes in the pie with a toothpick and pour hot water over the pie, letting it seep into the holes. Bake for about 1 hour, or until apples are tender and crust is golden brown.

Mrs. Nina Kay, New City, NY

MINCEY APPLE COBBLER

Yield: 6-8 servings

▼▼▼▼▼▼▼▼▼▼▼▼▼▼▼▼▼▼▼▼▼▼

1¼ CUPS WATER
GRATED RIND AND JUICE FROM ½ LEMON
5 CUPS APPLES, PEELED, CORED, AND CHOPPED (APPROXIMATELY 5 MEDIUM-SIZED APPLES)
2 TABLESPOONS CORNSTARCH
¾ CUP SUGAR
¼ TEASPOON CINNAMON
1 CUP PREPARED MINCEMEAT
10-OUNCE CAN REFRIGERATED FLAKY BISCUITS
3 TABLESPOONS MELTED MARGARINE
2 TABLESPOONS SUGAR
¼ TEASPOON CINNAMON

In a deep, 10-inch skillet, combine water, grated lemon rind and juice, and apples. Simmer on medium heat for 5 minutes. Remove from heat. Combine cornstarch, sugar, and cinnamon. Stir into apple mixture. Add mincemeat and mix well. Cook until mixture is hot and bubbly.

Preheat oven to 375° F. Separate biscuit dough into 10 biscuits. Using a doughnut cutter, cut center out of each biscuit. Place "doughnuts" around outer edge of apple mixture; arrange "holes" in center. Brush with melted margarine. Mix together sugar and cinnamon. Sprinkle over "doughnuts" and "holes." Bake for 35-40 minutes, or until topping is deep golden brown and apples are tender. Serve with cream, if desired.

Marie Balhiser, Salem, OR

APPLE COBBLER

Yield: 6 servings

▼▼▼▼▼▼▼▼▼▼▼▼▼▼▼▼▼▼▼▼▼

1¼ CUPS ALL-PURPOSE FLOUR
3 TABLESPOONS SUGAR
3 TEASPOONS BAKING POWDER
¼ TEASPOON SALT
⅓ CUP VEGETABLE SHORTENING
1 EGG
½ CUP MILK
3 MEDIUM-SIZE APPLES
⅓ CUP SUGAR
1 TEASPOON GRATED LEMON RIND
¾ CUP WATER
½ TEASPOON CINNAMON

Preheat oven to 375° F.

Sift together flour, sugar, baking powder, and salt. Cut shortening in with pastry blender. Mix in egg and milk. Stir with a fork to make a drop batter.

Peel, core, and slice apples. In a saucepan, combine apples, sugar, lemon rind, water, and cinnamon. Bring to a boil. Stir. Simmer until apples begin to soften. Pour into a 1½-quart casserole. Drop batter from a spoon onto hot fruit mixture. Bake for 25-30 minutes. Serve warm with cream.

Mrs. Peter Birmingham, Cedar Hill, MO

MOM'S APPLE COBBLER
Yield: 8 servings

▼▼▼▼▼▼▼▼▼▼▼▼▼▼▼▼▼▼▼▼▼

½ CUP MARGARINE OR BUTTER

2 CUPS SUGAR

2 CUPS WATER

½ CUP VEGETABLE SHORTENING

1½ CUPS SELF-RISING FLOUR

½ CUP MILK

1 TEASPOON CINNAMON

2 CUPS FINELY CHOPPED APPLES

Preheat oven to 350° F. Melt butter in a 13" x 9" x 2" baking dish or sheet cake pan. In a saucepan, heat sugar and water until sugar dissolves.

Cut shortening into flour until particles are like fine crumbs. Add milk and stir with a fork until dough leaves sides of bowl. Turn out onto slightly floured pastry cloth. Knead until smooth. Roll dough into a large rectangle about ¼ inch thick.

Sprinkle cinnamon over apples. Spread apples over dough. Roll up like a jelly roll. Dampen edges of dough with a little water and slice dough into ½-inch thick pieces (approximately 16 slices). Place in dish with melted butter. Pour sugar mixture over slices (crust will absorb liquid.) Bake for 55-60 minutes.

Toledo Alford, Barbourville, KY

ENGLISH APPLE PIE

Yield: 8 servings

▼▼▼▼▼▼▼▼▼▼▼▼▼▼▼▼▼▼▼▼▼

½ CUP BUTTER

½ CUP FIRMLY PACKED BROWN SUGAR

1 CUP ALL-PURPOSE FLOUR

2 TEASPOONS CINNAMON

3 TABLESPOONS WATER

½ CUP CHOPPED PECANS

4-5 LARGE COOKING APPLES, PEELED AND SLICED (APPROXIMATELY 6 CUPS)

½ CUP GRANULATED SUGAR

Preheat oven to 375° F.

Beat butter and brown sugar with wooden spoon or electric mixer until pale and fluffy. Stir in flour, 1 teaspoon cinnamon, and water. Mix until smooth and thick. Stir in pecans.

Mound apples in a 9-inch pie plate. Mix granulated sugar with remaining cinnamon. Sprinkle over apples. Spoon pecan mixture over apples in dollops. Bake for 45-50 minutes, or until apples are tender.

Kenney Yoder, Richmond, KY

CRANBERRY-APPLE NUT PIE

Yield: 8 servings

▼▼▼▼▼▼▼▼▼▼▼▼▼▼▼▼▼▼▼▼▼▼▼

2 CUPS CHOPPED FRESH CRANBERRIES
2 CUPS PEELED AND CHOPPED APPLES
1-1½ CUPS SUGAR
½ CUP CHOPPED NUTS
2 TABLESPOONS QUICK TAPIOCA
¼ TEASPOON CINNAMON
PASTRY FOR TWO 9-INCH PIE CRUSTS
MILK
SUGAR

Preheat oven to 375° F.

In a large bowl, combine cranberries, apples, sugar, nuts, tapioca, and cinnamon. Let stand 20 minutes.

Put apple mixture into pie crust. Adjust top crust, seal, and flute edges. Cut vents into top crust and brush with milk and sprinkle with sugar. Cover edges of pie with aluminum foil and bake for 25 minutes. Remove foil and continue to bake for 20-30 minutes more or until golden.

Linda E. Clary, Lincoln, NE

DUTCH APPLE-RASPBERRY PIE

Yield: 6 servings

▼▼▼▼▼▼▼▼▼▼▼▼▼▼▼▼▼▼▼▼

1 EGG YOLK
ONE GRAHAM CRACKER PIE CRUST

FILLING:

4-5 CUPS THINLY SLICED CORTLAND APPLES
½ CUP GRANULATED SUGAR
2 TEASPOONS CINNAMON
1 TEASPOON LEMON JUICE (OPTIONAL)
¼ TEASPOON NUTMEG (OPTIONAL)
2 TABLESPOONS BUTTER
2 TABLESPOONS ALL-PURPOSE FLOUR
1-1½ CUPS FRESH, RED RASPBERRIES
BUTTER

TOPPING:

½ CUP ALL-PURPOSE FLOUR
¼ CUP ROLLED OATS
1 CUP FIRMLY PACKED BROWN SUGAR
1 TEASPOON CINNAMON
½ CUP BUTTER
¼ TEASPOON SALT

Preheat oven to 400° F. Brush egg yolk onto pie crust and bake for 5 minutes. Remove from oven and reduce heat to 350° F.

For filling, in a large mixing bowl, combine apples, ½ cup granulated sugar, cinnamon, lemon juice, nutmeg, butter, and 2 tablespoons flour. Toss gently until mixed. Add raspberries and toss gently. Fill pie crust with apple mixture. Dot with butter.

For topping, in a small bowl, mix ½ cup flour, oats, brown sugar, cinnamon, ½ cup butter, and salt with a fork. Spread over apple mixture and bake for 30-40 minutes, or until apples are tender and topping is browned. Remove from oven and cool. Center will drop after cooling.

Linda S. Ochs, Waterloo, NY

APPLE-BLUEBERRY PIE

Yield: 6 servings

▼▼▼▼▼▼▼▼▼▼▼▼▼▼▼▼▼▼▼▼▼▼▼

⅔ CUP SUGAR

2 TABLESPOONS ALL-PURPOSE FLOUR

⅛ TEASPOON SALT

1 TEASPOON LEMON JUICE

¼ TEASPOON NUTMEG

½ TEASPOON CINNAMON

PASTRY FOR TWO 9-INCH PIE CRUSTS

6-7 CUPS THINLY SLICED APPLES (APPROXIMATELY 5 MEDIUM-SIZED APPLES)

1½ CUPS BLUEBERRIES

1 TABLESPOON BUTTER (NO MARGARINE)

Preheat oven to 425° F.

Mix all ingredients, except apples, blueberries, and butter to make a crust. Line bottom of a 9-inch pie plate with half the crust, and fill with half of the apples. Sprinkle with half of the sugar mixture. Spread blueberries over apples. Top with remaining apples, heaping them in the center. Sprinkle remaining sugar mixture over top and dot with butter. Put on top crust and slash through a few places to make vents. Bake for 40-50 minutes, or until crust is nicely browned and filling is tender. (Cover edges with aluminum foil to prevent them from getting too brown.)

Jolene Schoettelkotte, Amelia, OH

RICHARD'S APPLE-BLACKBERRY PIE

Yield: 6 servings

▼▼▼▼▼▼▼▼▼▼▼▼▼▼▼▼▼▼▼▼

PASTRY FOR TWO 9-INCH PIE CRUSTS
3 TABLESPOONS MELTED BUTTER (NO MARGARINE)
5 CUPS PEELED AND SLICED JONATHAN OR GRANNY SMITH APPLES
2 CUPS BLACKBERRIES
½ CUP GRANULATED SUGAR
¼ CUP BROWN SUGAR
4 TABLESPOONS ALL-PURPOSE FLOUR
2 TEASPOONS FRESHLY SQUEEZED LEMON JUICE
MILK

Preheat oven to 350° F.
Prepare and roll out pastry. Line a 9-inch pie pan with pastry.
In a bowl, blend butter and all other ingredients except milk. Mix gently. Pour mixture into pie crust. Cover with second pie crust that has been vented with a fork. Bake for 20 minutes. Brush top with milk. Increase heat to 375° F. and bake for 20 minutes more, or until crust is golden brown.

Richard E. Cheli, Owensboro, KY

ORANGE-APPLE PIE

Yield: 6-8 servings

This fruit pie recipe contains no salt and a minimum amount of sugar. To make the "dry" applesauce, I use Golden Delicious apples (peeled), no sugar, and a minimum amount of water—only enough to start the cooking. I cook until the apples have softened and then mash them with a potato masher to make a "lumpy" type of applesauce. This pie and others thickened with cornstarch should not be frozen.

▼▼▼▼▼▼▼▼▼▼▼▼▼▼▼▼▼▼▼▼▼▼

½ CUP SUGAR

½ CUP CORNSTARCH

3½ CUPS "DRY" APPLESAUCE

ONE 12-OUNCE CONTAINER FROZEN ORANGE JUICE CONCENTRATE, UNDILUTED

TWO 9-INCH PIE SHELLS, UNBAKED

Preheat oven to 450° F. Mix sugar and cornstarch thoroughly. Add "dry" applesauce and orange concentrate. Pour into pie shell. Top with second crust and flute. Cut slits in top crust. Bake for 10 minutes. Reduce heat to 350° F. and bake for 35-40 minutes more.

John Van Grouw, Franklin Lakes, NJ

AWESOME APPLE PIE

Yield: 8 servings

▼▼▼▼▼▼▼▼▼▼▼▼▼▼▼▼▼▼▼▼

CRUST:
1¾ CUPS ALL-PURPOSE FLOUR
1 TABLESPOON SUGAR
½ CUP CHILLED, UNSALTED BUTTER
1 EGG YOLK
2 TABLESPOONS ICE WATER

FILLING:
1½ POUNDS GRANNY SMITH APPLES
SUGAR
3 TABLESPOONS MELTED BUTTER
4 FRESH APRICOTS
4 TABLESPOONS APRICOT JAM
2 TABLESPOONS FRESH LEMON JUICE, OR 2 TABLESPOONS COINTREAU LIQUEUR

For crust, place flour and sugar in a mixing bowl. With two knifes, cut in butter until crumbly. Mix egg yolk and ice water together and add gradually to flour mixture. Form into a ball. Wrap in plastic wrap and chill for 1 hour.

Preheat oven to 400° F. Butter an 11- or 12-inch pie dish with removable bottom. On a floured surface, roll out dough to ³⁄₁₆-inch thickness, just to fit the pie dish. Prick with a fork. Line with aluminum foil and fill with dry beans. Bake for 15 minutes. Remove foil and beans and bake about 10 minutes more or until slightly browned. Cool.

Reduce heat to 320° F. Peel, core, and slice apples. Roll each slice in sugar and cook in melted butter until sugar has caramelized and is light brown. Repeat until all apples have been coated and cooked. Slice apricots and cook the same way as apples. Place on a plate to cool. Arrange fruit in concentric circles in pie crust until covered and all fruit is used. Heat apricot jam in a saucepan. Add lemon juice or Cointreau and spoon over fruit in pie crust. Bake for 15 minutes. Serve warm or at room temperature with fresh whipped cream.

Felicity Gatchell, Birmingham, AL

Peach, Pear, Plum, and Apricot Pies

▼▼▼

FRESH PEACH PIE

Yield: 8 servings

▼▼▼▼▼▼▼▼▼▼▼▼▼▼▼▼▼▼▼▼▼

JUICE OF 1 LEMON
3 CUPS SLICED FRESH PEACHES
1 EGG, BEATEN
⅓ CUP MELTED BUTTER
1 CUP SUGAR
⅓ CUP ALL-PURPOSE FLOUR
½ TEASPOON NUTMEG, PREFERABLY FRESHLY GROUND
1 TEASPOON VANILLA EXTRACT
ONE 9-INCH PIE SHELL, UNBAKED

Preheat oven to 350° F. Lightly toss lemon juice and peaches. Mix together egg, butter, sugar, flour, nutmeg, and vanilla. Place peaches in pie shell and pour egg mixture over peaches. Bake for 45-50 minutes. This recipe can also be doubled and baked in a 9" x 13" baking dish.

Kathy Whitten, Harrisonburg, VA

OLD-FASHIONED PEACH PIE

Yield: 6 servings

▼▼▼▼▼▼▼▼▼▼▼▼▼▼▼▼▼▼▼▼▼▼

¾ CUP SUGAR

3 TABLESPOONS ALL-PURPOSE FLOUR, OR 2¼ TABLESPOONS QUICK TAPIOCA

¼ TEASPOON CINNAMON

¼ TEASPOON NUTMEG

⅛ TEASPOON SALT

5 CUPS SLICED FRESH PEACHES

1 TEASPOON LEMON JUICE

¼ TEASPOON ALMOND EXTRACT

PASTRY FOR TWO 9-INCH PIE CRUSTS

2 TABLESPOONS BUTTER OR MARGARINE

Preheat oven to 425° F. Combine sugar, flour, cinnamon, nutmeg, and salt. Add to peaches. Sprinkle on lemon juice and almond extract. Pour into a pastry-lined 9-inch pie pan. Dot with butter. Adjust top crust, flute edges, and cut steam vents. Bake for 40-45 minutes, or until peaches are tender and crust is golden brown.

Patsy C. Anderson, Carroll, OH

PEACHES 'N' CREAM PIE

Yield: 6-8 servings

This pie has been a family favorite for almost 40 years.

▼▼▼▼▼▼▼▼▼▼▼▼▼▼▼▼▼▼▼▼▼

PASTRY FOR ONE 9-INCH OR 10-INCH PIE CRUST
6-8 RIPE PEACHES

SAUCE:
¾ CUP SUGAR
2 TABLESPOONS ALL-PURPOSE FLOUR
DASH SALT
DASH CINNAMON
1 CUP WHIPPING CREAM (NO SUBSTITUTES)
1 TEASPOON VANILLA EXTRACT

Preheat oven to 425° F.
Line a 9-inch or 10-inch pie plate with pastry. Slice peaches into crust until level with top of plate.
For sauce, stir together dry ingredients. Gradually stir in whipping cream and vanilla until well mixed. Pour sauce over peaches. (You may have a little sauce left over if you're using a 9-inch pie plate.)
Bake for 10 minutes. Reduce heat to 350° F. and bake 30 minutes more. (The filling may "shake" in the crust at the end of the baking.)

Joan R. Strom, Brookfield, IL

PEACH CREAM PIE

Yield: 6-8 servings

This recipe for Peach Cream Pie has been in our family for a long time. Several years ago mother wrote cookbooks for some family members. Included in the books are recipes for food we ate while growing up. At the end of each recipe she added comments about the source of the recipe, special occasions when it was served, and whose favorite it was. This pie is included in my cookbook because I've always liked it.

▼▼▼▼▼▼▼▼▼▼▼▼▼▼▼▼▼▼▼▼▼▼▼

ONE 9-INCH PIE SHELL, UNBAKED
2 TABLESPOONS BUTTER
3 CUPS SLICED FRESH PEACHES
⅔ CUP SUGAR
¼ CUP ALL-PURPOSE FLOUR
¼ TEASPOON NUTMEG
1 CUP HALF-AND-HALF OR CREAM

Preheat oven to 425° F. Dot pie shell with butter. Cover with peaches. Combine dry ingredients and add half-and-half. Mix thoroughly and pour over peaches. Bake for 35-40 minutes.

Pat Smart, Murphysboro, IL

INDIANA CREAMY PEACH PIE

Yield: 8 servings

In the fifteen years I have been married, I have rolled, stirred, experimented, sweated, cried, and rejoiced over many different pie recipes. It is my hope that some day when I'm long gone, my great-great-great-grandchildren will enjoy "Grandma Scher's Creamy Peach Pie!"

▼▼▼▼▼▼▼▼▼▼▼▼▼▼▼▼▼▼▼▼

CRUST:
1½ CUPS ALL-PURPOSE FLOUR
½ TEASPOON SALT
½ CUP BUTTER

FILLING:
4 CUPS SLICED FRESH PEACHES
1 CUP SUGAR
2½ TABLESPOONS ALL-PURPOSE FLOUR

1 EGG
¼ TEASPOON SALT
1 TEASPOON VANILLA EXTRACT
1 CUP SOUR CREAM

TOPPING:
⅓ CUP SUGAR
⅓ CUP ALL-PURPOSE FLOUR
¼ CUP BUTTER

Preheat oven to 400° F.

For crust, combine flour and salt and cut in butter. Press into a 9-inch pie plate.

For filling, put peaches into a bowl. Sprinkle with ¼ cup sugar and set aside. In another bowl, combine remaining sugar, 2½ tablespoons flour, egg, salt, and vanilla. Fold in sour cream. Stir mixture into peaches. Pour into crust. Bake for 15 minutes. Reduce heat to 350° F. and bake 20 minutes more.

Prepare topping by combining all ingredients until crumbly. After baking at 350° F. for 20 minutes, sprinkle topping evenly on top. Bake for 10 minutes more at 400° F.

Anne Marie Scher, Coatesville, PA

OPEN-FACED PEACH CREAM PIE

Yield: 6 servings

This recipe was brought from Germany by my grandmother when she immigrated at the age of 17 in the mid-1800s. It's been a family favorite ever since.

▼▼▼▼▼▼▼▼▼▼▼▼▼▼▼▼▼▼▼▼▼

4 TABLESPOONS ALL-PURPOSE FLOUR
1 TABLESPOON PLUS ¾ CUP SUGAR
ONE 9-INCH PIE SHELL, UNBAKED
DASH SALT
¾ CUP MILK
9-10 MEDIUM-SIZE FRESH PEACHES, SLICED
CINNAMON
MARGARINE OR BUTTER

Preheat oven to 450° F. Mix together 1 tablespoon flour and 1 tablespoon sugar. "Dust" the bottom of pie shell to help prevent it from getting soggy. Mix remaining flour, ¾ cup sugar, and salt. Add milk and mix. Pour over peaches in pie shell. Sprinkle with cinnamon. Dot with margarine or butter. Bake for 10 minutes. Reduce heat to 350° F. and continue baking for 45 minutes more. Serve slightly warm.

Mrs. D.P. Workman, Mt. Vernon, OH

LOW-CHOLESTEROL PEACH PIE

Yield: 6 servings

▼▼▼▼▼▼▼▼▼▼▼▼▼▼▼▼▼▼▼▼

4 CUPS PEELED AND SLICED FRESH PEACHES
2 TABLESPOONS HONEY OR BROWN SUGAR
2 EGG WHITES, WELL BEATEN
1 TABLESPOON TAPIOCA
1 CUP WHOLE WHEAT FLOUR
1 TEASPOON BAKING SODA
1 TABLESPOON NO-CHOLESTEROL SPREAD OR MARGARINE, AT ROOM TEMPERATURE
⅓ CUP COLD WATER

CUSTARD:
4 EGG SUBSTITUTES
⅓ CUP HONEY OR BROWN SUGAR
2 TEASPOONS VANILLA EXTRACT
2 CUPS SKIM MILK

Preheat oven to 425° F.

Mix peaches, honey or brown sugar, egg whites, and tapioca together and spread over an oiled or sprayed 9-inch square baking dish. Mix flour, baking soda, and spread or margarine. Add cold water. Knead to a consistency that can be rolled, and roll out on floured surface to 9 inch square and ½ inch thick. Place over peaches and prick the top. Bake for 20-30 minutes.

For custard, beat eggs, honey or brown sugar, and vanilla. Bring milk to a boil and add milk, a little at a time, to egg mixture. Return milk mixture to the saucepan and cook on low heat, stirring with wooden spoon until thick. Serve custard spooned over peach pie.

Felicity J. Gatchell, Birmingham, AL

PEACH PRALINE PIE

Yield: 6-8 servings

▼▼▼▼▼▼▼▼▼▼▼▼▼▼▼▼▼▼▼▼▼▼

4 CUPS PEELED AND SLICED PEACHES
¾ CUP GRANULATED SUGAR
1½ TEASPOONS CORNSTARCH
1½ TEASPOONS LEMON JUICE
¼ CUP ALL-PURPOSE FLOUR
⅓ CUP FIRMLY PACKED BROWN SUGAR
½ CUP CHOPPED PECANS
3 TABLESPOONS BUTTER
ONE 9-INCH PIE SHELL, UNBAKED

Preheat oven to 425° F. Combine peaches, granulated sugar, cornstarch, and lemon juice in a bowl and mix together. Combine flour, brown sugar, and pecans in a small bowl. Mix butter into flour mixture until crumbly. Sprinkle one-third of pecan mixture on bottom of pie shell. Cover with peach mixture. Sprinkle remaining pecan mixture on top. Bake for 15 minutes. Reduce heat to 350° F. and continue baking for 30 minutes more.

Eva Schroeder, Rock Port, MO

PEACH CRUMB PIE

Yield: 8 servings

▼▼▼▼▼▼▼▼▼▼▼▼▼▼▼▼▼▼▼▼▼▼

FILLING:

1 CUP SUGAR
2 TABLESPOONS ALL-PURPOSE FLOUR
10 PEACHES, SLICED (APPROXIMATELY 6 CUPS)
ONE 9-INCH PIE SHELL, UNBAKED

TOPPING:

¾ CUP ALL-PURPOSE FLOUR
¾ CUP SUGAR
¼ CUP BUTTER
½ TEASPOON GROUND GINGER

Preheat oven to 350° F. For filling, mix together sugar and flour and mix with peaches. Fill pie shell with peach mixture. For topping, in a small bowl, mix together all topping ingredients until mixture breaks into crumbs. Sprinkle crumb mixture thickly over peaches. Bake for 35 minutes.

Helen West, Tucson, AR

ZWIEBACK PEACH TORTE

Yield: 10 servings

This recipe has been a family favorite for 13 years, ever since I found it in the attic of my grandma's house. It was originally written in 1930 and has that delicious, old-time flavor, familiar yet unique.

▼▼▼▼▼▼▼▼▼▼▼▼▼▼▼▼▼▼▼▼▼

16 SLICES ZWIEBACK CRACKERS, CRUSHED
2 CUPS SLICED FRESH PEACHES
2 EGGS, BEATEN
½ CUP SOUR CREAM
⅔ CUP SUGAR
2 TEASPOONS VANILLA EXTRACT
⅛ TEASPOON CINNAMON

Preheat oven to 375° F. (350° F. for glass pan). Place two-thirds of zwieback crumbs in a well-buttered, 8-inch cake pan. Cover with peaches. Mix eggs, sour cream, sugar, vanilla, and cinnamon. Pour egg mixture over peaches. Sprinkle with remaining crumbs. Bake for 20 minutes. Serve warm with vanilla ice cream.

Alternate: Apples or canned peaches can be substituted. This torte fits in a 9" x 13" pan, doubled.

Janet Crawford, Gold Hill, OR

PEACH STREUSEL PIE
Yield: 8 servings

▼▼▼▼▼▼▼▼▼▼▼▼▼▼▼▼▼▼▼▼▼

FILLING:

5 CUPS PEELED AND THICKLY SLICED BURBANK JULY ELBERTA PEACHES
ONE 9-INCH PIE SHELL, UNBAKED
⅓ CUP HONEY
1 EGG
2 TABLESPOONS CREAM
2 TABLESPOONS ALL-PURPOSE FLOUR
1 TEASPOON VANILLA EXTRACT

TOPPING:

¼ CUP FIRMLY PACKED BROWN SUGAR
½ CUP ALL-PURPOSE FLOUR
¼ CUP BUTTER, AT ROOM TEMPERATURE
½ CUP CHOPPED MISSOURI HARDY PECANS

Preheat oven to 400° F.

For filling, arrange peaches in pie shell. Beat together honey, egg, cream, flour, and vanilla. Pour mixture evenly over peaches.

For topping, mix brown sugar, ½ cup flour, butter, and pecans until crumbly. Sprinkle over peaches in pie shell. Bake for about 45 minutes or until browned and bubbly.

Maureen Patricia Darby, Lebanon, MO

DOUBLE PEACH COBBLER

Yield: 16 servings

▼▼▼▼▼▼▼▼▼▼▼▼▼▼▼▼▼▼▼▼

2½ CUPS PEELED AND SLICED PEACHES

1½ CUPS ALL-PURPOSE FLOUR

2 TABLESPOONS OAT BRAN

⅓ CUP FIRMLY PACKED BROWN SUGAR

2½ TEASPOONS BAKING POWDER

¼ TEASPOON CINNAMON

¾ CUP MILK

1 CUP PEELED AND DICED PEACHES

⅓ CUP MILD HONEY OR GRANULATED SUGAR

⅔ CUP BOILING WATER

4 TABLESPOONS MARGARINE

Preheat oven to 350° F. Lightly spray a 9" x 9" x 2" baking dish with a nonstick spray. Arrange sliced peaches on bottom of baking dish. Set aside.

In a mixing bowl, thoroughly combine flour, oat bran, brown sugar, baking powder, and cinnamon. Add milk and stir to mix. Add diced peaches. Mix until just combined; do *not* beat. Drop by spoonfuls over sliced peaches in baking dish.

In a small saucepan, heat honey or granulated sugar with boiling water and margarine until honey or sugar and margarine melt. Spoon hot mixture carefully over batter. Gently lift edges of batter, if necessary, in order to use all of the hot mixture. Do *not* mix with batter. Bake 40 minutes, or until tester inserted in center comes out clean. Remove from oven to a wire rack to cool. Cut into 16 squares to serve. This is best served cold, but may be served warm with whipped topping. If serving warm, increase *both* brown sugar and honey or granulated sugar to ½ cup *each*. Apricots or pears may be used in place of peaches.

Eileene Johnson, Clifton, CO

EASY PEACH COBBLER

Yield: 8 servings

▼▼▼▼▼▼▼▼▼▼▼▼▼▼▼▼▼▼▼▼▼

1 STICK MARGARINE
1 CUP SELF-RISING FLOUR
1 CUP SUGAR
1 CUP MILK
3 CUPS SLICED FRESH PEACHES (OR MORE TO TASTE)

Preheat oven to 375° F. Put margarine in a 9" x 6" baking pan or dish. Place in oven until margarine melts.

Stir together flour and sugar. Add milk all at once. Stir just to blend. Spread melted margarine evenly over bottom of baking dish. Pour half of the batter over margarine. Arrange peaches on top of batter. Add remaining batter, spreading evenly over peaches. Bake for about 45 minutes or until lightly browned.

Deanna Rice, Golden, CO

FRESH PEACH COBBLER

Yield: 5 servings

▼▼▼▼▼▼▼▼▼▼▼▼▼▼▼▼▼▼▼▼▼

6 CUPS SLICED FRESH, FULLY RIPE PEACHES

1 TABLESPOON LEMON JUICE

¼ CUP GRANULATED SUGAR

¼ CUP PACKED BROWN SUGAR

1½ TABLESPOONS CORNSTARCH

½ CUP WATER

⅛ TEASPOON CINNAMON

⅛ TEASPOON ALLSPICE

⅛ TEASPOON NUTMEG

½ CUP GRANULATED SUGAR

½ CUP ALL-PURPOSE FLOUR

½ TEASPOON BAKING POWDER

¼ TEASPOON SALT

2 TABLESPOONS MARGARINE

1 LARGE EGG

1 TEASPOON GRANULATED SUGAR

Preheat oven to 350° F. Grease a 2-quart casserole.

Combine peaches and lemon juice and pour in casserole. Sprinkle with the ¼ cup granulated sugar. Mix together brown sugar, cornstarch, water, and spices and cook on medium heat until thickened. Pour over peaches. Combine ½ cup granulated sugar, flour, baking powder, salt, margarine, and egg, and mix together. Spread on top of casserole. Sprinkle 1 teaspoon granulated sugar on top of crust. Bake for 40-45 minutes, or until top browns.

Nancy R. Crews, Hurt, VA

PEACH COBBLER RING

Yield: 8 servings

▼▼▼▼▼▼▼▼▼▼▼▼▼▼▼▼▼▼▼▼▼▼▼

CRUST:

2 CUPS ALL-PURPOSE FLOUR
4 TEASPOONS BAKING POWDER
1 TABLESPOON GRANULATED SUGAR
½ TEASPOON SALT
½ CUP VEGETABLE SHORTENING
⅔ CUP MILK

FILLING:

2 TABLESPOONS BUTTER, AT ROOM
TEMPERATURE
¼ CUP BROWN SUGAR
1 TABLESPOON ALL-PURPOSE FLOUR
1 TEASPOON CINNAMON
2 CUPS DICED FRESH PEACHES
BUTTER

Preheat oven to 400° F.

For crust, sift dry ingredients together and cut in shortening until mixture resembles coarse crumbs. Add milk and stir to form a soft dough. Turn out on lightly floured surface and knead 6-8 times. Roll into an 18" x 9" rectangle.

For filling, spread dough with butter and sprinkle with a mixture of brown sugar, flour, and cinnamon. Cover with peaches. Roll up like a jelly roll. Place on an ungreased baking sheet and form into a circle. Make slits from outside edge of circle almost to the center (just on top of the circle) every 2 inches. Turn each cut into each side. Brush lightly with butter or milk. Bake for 25-30 minutes. Serve warm with milk or cream and peaches, if desired.

Mrs. Erma Yutzy, Drakesville, IA

PEACH COBBLER PIE

Yield: 8-10 servings

▼▼▼▼▼▼▼▼▼▼▼▼▼▼▼▼▼▼▼▼▼▼▼

½ CUP BUTTER OR MARGARINE
2 CUPS SUGAR
2 CUPS WATER
½ CUP VEGETABLE SHORTENING
1½ CUP SELF-RISING FLOUR
⅓ CUP MILK
½ TEASPOON NUTMEG
2 CUPS FINELY SLICED PEACHES

Preheat oven to 350° F. Melt butter in a 13" x 9" x 2" baking dish. In a saucepan, heat sugar and water until sugar dissolves.

Cut shortening into flour until it is crumbly. Add milk and stir with a fork until the dough leaves the side of the bowl. Turn dough out onto a lightly floured surface or pastry cloth. Knead just until smooth. Roll dough into a large rectangle, ¼ inch thick. Sprinkle nutmeg over dough and place peaches in a layer over dough. Roll dough up like a jelly roll. Slice dough in 16 pieces, ½ inch thick. Place in baking dish with melted butter. Pour sugar syrup over pieces. This looks like too much liquid, but the crust will absorb it. Bake for 1 hour. (Other fruits may be used.)

Mrs. Edna Shipley, Hartsville, AL

DEEP-DISH PEACHY-PEAR PIE

Yield: 9 servings

Although I grew up in the country during the Depression, Mother could go out into the orchard or berry patch and "invent" desserts that were the envy of the neighborhood and certainly us four youngsters. I treasure every one of her recipes.

▼▼▼▼▼▼▼▼▼▼▼▼▼▼▼▼▼▼▼▼▼

PASTRY FOR ONE 9-INCH PIE CRUST
2 CUPS SUGAR
½ CUP ALL-PURPOSE FLOUR
½ TEASPOON CINNAMON
½ TEASPOON MACE
6 CUPS PEELED AND SLICED FRESH PEACHES
2 CUPS PEELED AND SLICED FRESH PEARS
3 TABLESPOONS BUTTER

Preheat oven to 400° F.

Combine sugar, flour, cinnamon, and mace. Fold sugar mixture gently into peaches and pears. Pour into a buttered, 9-inch square pan and dot with butter.

Roll pastry into a 12-inch square. Place pastry over filling. Fold edge of crust under and flute against inside of pan. Cut several slits for steam vents. Bake for about 50 minutes or until a light brown. Serve warm or cold with whipped cream or vanilla ice cream.

Muriel Looney, Eugene, OR

FRESH PEAR PIE

Yield: 6-8 servings

▼▼▼▼▼▼▼▼▼▼▼▼▼▼▼▼▼▼▼▼▼▼▼

½ CUP SUGAR

2 TABLESPOONS CORNSTARCH

¼ TEASPOON CINNAMON

¼ TEASPOON MACE

½ CUP WATER

1 TABLESPOON LEMON JUICE

1 TABLESPOON BUTTER

4 CUPS PEELED AND SLICED PEARS

TWO 9-INCH PIE SHELLS, UNBAKED

SUGAR

Preheat oven to 400° F. Combine   cup sugar, cornstarch, cinnamon, and mace. Stir in water, lemon juice, and butter. Stir over medium-high heat until mixture begins to thicken. Add pears. Remove from heat. Pour into pie shell. Put the top crust in place, seal the edge, and make slits in the top to release steam. Bake for 20 minutes. Sprinkle with sugar and bake 20 minutes more or until browned.

Janice Goodner, Macomb, OK

CREAMY BRANDY PEAR PIE
Yield: 8 servings

▼▼▼▼▼▼▼▼▼▼▼▼▼▼▼▼▼▼▼▼

6 ASIAN PEARS (OR ENOUGH TO MAKE 6 CUPS)
¼ CUP SUGAR
¼ CUP HONEY
¼ CUP WATER
½ CUP APPLE BRANDY
PINCH CINNAMON
PINCH NUTMEG
PINCH PAPRIKA
TWO 9-INCH PIE SHELLS, UNBAKED
½ CUP WHIPPING CREAM

Preheat oven to 400° F.

Peel and core pears, slice thinly. Combine pears, sugar, honey, water, brandy, and spices in a saucepan and simmer until pears are barely tender. Stir several times with a wooden spoon. Drain pears and put into pie shell. Wet edges of crust with water, and place top crust on pears, sealing edges with a fork. Cut three vents in the top crust. Bake for 40 minutes. Remove from oven. Pour whipping cream through vent holes and return to oven for 10-15 minutes, or until pears are tender to a fork and crust is browned. Serve warm.

W. Joe and Lucy R. Robertson, Corpus Christi, TX

PEAR CUSTARD PIE

Yield: 6 servings

▼▼▼▼▼▼▼▼▼▼▼▼▼▼▼▼▼▼▼▼▼▼

4 FULLY RIPE, MEDIUM-SIZED BARTLETT PEARS

LEMON JUICE

ONE 9-INCH PIE SHELL, UNBAKED

1 CUP SUGAR

¼ CUP ALL-PURPOSE FLOUR

¼ CUP BUTTER OR MARGARINE, AT ROOM TEMPERATURE

3 EGGS

1 TEASPOON VANILLA EXTRACT

⅛ TEASPOON SALT

Preheat oven to 350° F. Peel and core pears. Brush with lemon juice and arrange in pie shell, cutting pears in halves and quarters to fit. Thoroughly blend together sugar, flour, butter, eggs, vanilla, and salt. Pour sugar mixture over pears. Bake for 45 minutes, or until custard is set. Cool at least 1 hour before serving.

Mrs. M.J. Mosier, Auburn, KS

BATTER-CRUST DAMSON PLUM PIE

Yield: 6 servings

I like to serve this dessert warm, with whipped topping.

▼▼▼▼▼▼▼▼▼▼▼▼▼▼▼▼▼▼▼▼▼▼

2 CUPS DAMSON PLUMS
2 CUPS SUGAR
1 STICK BUTTER, MELTED
1 CUP SIFTED, SELF-RISING FLOUR
½ CUP MILK

Preheat oven to 350° F. Boil plums with 1 cup sugar. Melt butter in a baking dish. Combine flour with remaining sugar and milk and mix well. Pour batter into melted butter. Pour hot fruit over batter and bake for 45 minutes or until browned on top.

Mary Pierce, St. Clair Shores, MI

APRICOT PIE WITH TENDER OATMEAL CRUST

Yield: 6-8 servings

▼▼▼▼▼▼▼▼▼▼▼▼▼▼▼▼▼▼▼▼▼▼

FILLING:

5 CUPS PEELED AND HALVED APRICOTS
¾ CUP SUGAR
3 TABLESPOONS ALL-PURPOSE FLOUR
¼ TEASPOON NUTMEG (OPTIONAL)
2 TABLESPOONS MARGARINE

CRUST:

1 CUP ROLLED OATS (OLD-FASHIONED OR QUICK)
1 CUP ALL-PURPOSE FLOUR
⅔ CUP MARGARINE
6 TABLESPOONS COLD WATER

Preheat oven to 400° F.

For filling, place apricots in a bowl. Combine other filling ingredients. Add this mixture to apricots and mix lightly.

For crust, blend oats in a dry blender until they look like flour. Mix together the oats and 1 cup flour. Cut margarine in with pastry blender or two knives until mixture is evenly grainy. Add cold water and stir until a ball is formed. Divide in half, and roll out bottom and top crusts between wax paper. Place bottom crust in a 9-inch pie pan.

Fill crust with apricot mixture and top with crust or lattice (twisted strips in a diamond pattern are easy and attractive). Trim and crimp edges to seal top to bottom. Bake for 40-45 minutes or until golden brown.

Mary Jo Kearns, Valley Falls, KS

DELECTABLE APRICOT PIE

Yield: 8 servings

▼▼▼▼▼▼▼▼▼▼▼▼▼▼▼▼▼▼▼▼▼▼▼▼

PASTRY FOR TWO 9-INCH PIE CRUSTS
4 CUPS QUARTERED FRESH APRICOTS (FIRM BUT RIPE)
1 CUP SUGAR
2 ½ TABLESPOONS MINUTE TAPIOCA
¼ TEASPOON CINNAMON
¼ TEASPOON NUTMEG

Preheat oven to 425° F. Prepare pastry for a 9-inch pie pan.

Mix remaining ingredients and let stand for 5 minutes. Pour into pie crust and cover with top crust. Slit top crust. Bake for 15 minutes. Reduce heat to 350° F. and bake for 45 minutes more. (This pie may be frozen in unbaked pie crust and then baked as above for a special treat.)

Debra Lynne Olson, Salt Lake City, UT

APRICOT DELIGHT

Yield: 6-8 servings

▼▼▼▼▼▼▼▼▼▼▼▼▼▼▼▼▼▼▼▼▼

CRUST:

¼ CUP MARGARINE, AT ROOM TEMPERATURE

¼ CUP SUGAR

1 EGG YOLK

1 CUP ALL-PURPOSE FLOUR

FILLING:

½ CUP SUGAR

3 TABLESPOONS CORNSTARCH

1½ CUPS ORANGE JUICE

¼ CUP LEMON JUICE

1 TEASPOON GRATED LEMON RIND

6 CUPS QUARTERED FRESH APRICOTS

WHIPPED CREAM

Preheat oven to 400° F.

For crust, mix together margarine, ¼ cup sugar, and egg yolk. Mix in flour with pastry blender until crumbs form. Press firmly into a 9-inch pie plate. Bake for 8 minutes. Cool.

For filling, combine ½ cup sugar and cornstarch in a saucepan and gradually stir in orange juice until smooth. Stirring constantly, bring to a boil and cook for 1 minute. Remove from heat and stir in lemon juice and lemon rind. Cool. Fold in apricots and pile onto pie shell. Top with whipped cream.

Charmaine Kerchner, Goodrich, MI

APRICOT COBBLER

Yield: 6-8 servings

▼▼▼▼▼▼▼▼▼▼▼▼▼▼▼▼▼▼▼▼

PASTRY FOR TWO 8-INCH PIE CRUSTS
2 QUARTS FRESH APRICOTS, HALVED AND PITTED
1 CUP SUGAR
1 TEASPOON CINNAMON
½ TEASPOON NUTMEG
3 TABLESPOONS ALL-PURPOSE FLOUR
2 TABLESPOONS BUTTER OR MARGARINE

Preheat oven to 375° F. Line an 8" x 8" square baking dish with pie pastry and put in apricots. Mix together sugar, spices, and flour. Sprinkle sugar mixture on top of apricots. Dot with butter or margarine. Cover with top pastry; make slits in it to let steam escape. Bake for 50-60 minutes.

Yvonna Harris, Springfield, OH

RHUBARB PIES

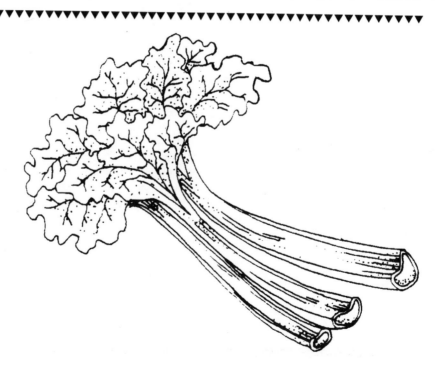

SUPERB RHUBARB PIE

Yield: 6 servings

▼▼▼▼▼▼▼▼▼▼▼▼▼▼▼▼▼▼▼▼▼▼

3 EGGS
1¼ CUPS SUGAR
¼ CUP MARGARINE OR BUTTER
¼ TEASPOON SALT
¼ CUP ALL-PURPOSE FLOUR
2½ CUPS CHOPPED RHUBARB
ONE 10-INCH PIE SHELL, UNBAKED

Preheat oven to 375° F.

Separate eggs. Beat together egg whites and ¼ cup sugar until stiff. Set aside.

Mix thoroughly egg yolks, margarine or butter, salt, remaining sugar, and flour. Fold in rhubarb, and then reserved meringue. Pile into pie shell. Bake on bottom rack for 15 minutes. Reduce heat to 325° F. and bake for 30 minutes more. Serve at room temperature.

Christine L. DiPirro, Orchard Park, NY

RHUBARB PIE
Yield: 6 servings

I've never shared this pie recipe before, not because it is a family secret, but because it is so simple and plain. But in my family, we like to taste the fruit, so my pies are fruit—no spices or fancy additives. This pie may not be fancy, but it lives up to its name.

▼▼▼▼▼▼▼▼▼▼▼▼▼▼▼▼▼▼▼▼▼▼

1 CUP SUGAR
¼ CUP QUICK TAPIOCA
5 CUPS CUBED RHUBARB
PASTRY FOR TWO 9-INCH PIE CRUSTS

Preheat oven to 425° F. Toss first three ingredients together. Turn into a pastry-lined 9-inch pie pan. Cover with second crust. Prick top crust all over with a fork. Bake for 45 minutes, or until crust is browned.

Cynthia Johnston, Lebanon, PA

LINDA D'S RUBY RHUBARB PIE

Yield: 6-8 servings

▼▼▼▼▼▼▼▼▼▼▼▼▼▼▼▼▼▼▼▼

3 EGGS
1¼ CUPS SUGAR
¼ CUP BUTTER (NO MARGARINE)
3 TABLESPOONS UNDILUTED FROZEN ORANGE JUICE
¼ CUP ALL-PURPOSE FLOUR
¼ TEASPOON SALT
2½ CUPS DICED RUBY RED RHUBARB
¾ TEASPOON NUTMEG
ONE 9-INCH PIE SHELL, UNBAKED

Preheat oven to 375° F.

Separate eggs. Beat egg whites until stiff. Beat in ¼ cup sugar and set aside.

Combine butter, orange juice, flour, salt, egg yolks, and remaining sugar. Beat well. Add rhubarb and nutmeg. Stir. Fold rhubarb mixture into beaten egg whites. Put into pie shell. Place pie on bottom rack and bake for 15 minutes. Reduce heat to 325° F. and continue baking for 45 minutes more.

Linda Davinroy, Fairview Heights, IL

RHUBARB CUSTARD PIE

Yield: 6-8 servings

This recipe has been handed down in our family for years. It is a favorite always!

▼▼▼▼▼▼▼▼▼▼▼▼▼▼▼▼▼▼▼▼

FILLING:

2 CUPS DICED RHUBARB

1 CUP GRANULATED SUGAR

2 TABLESPOONS ALL-PURPOSE FLOUR

½ CUP MILK

2 EGGS, SLIGHTLY BEATEN

DASH SALT

DASH NUTMEG

ONE 9-INCH PIE SHELL, UNBAKED

TOPPING:

1 CUP BROWN SUGAR

3 TABLESPOONS BUTTER

1 HEAPING TABLESPOON ALL-PURPOSE FLOUR

DASH CINNAMON

Preheat oven to 425° F. For filling, mix filling ingredients and pour into pie shell. For topping, combine all topping ingredients and put on top of the filling. Bake for 20 minutes. Reduce heat to 375° and bake for 30 minutes more. Pie is done when the center is set.

Lera M. Zimmerman, Sandusky, OH

RHUBARB PINWHEEL PIE

Yield: 10 servings

▼▼▼▼▼▼▼▼▼▼▼▼▼▼▼▼▼▼▼▼▼▼

FILLING:

1 CUP SUGAR
4 TABLESPOONS ALL-PURPOSE FLOUR
¼ TEASPOON SALT
6 CUPS DICED RHUBARB
4 TABLESPOONS BUTTER

PINWHEELS:

1 CUP ALL-PURPOSE FLOUR
¼ TEASPOON SALT
¼ TEASPOON BAKING POWDER
2 TABLESPOONS SUGAR
½ CUP PLUS **2** TABLESPOONS BUTTER
2-3 TABLESPOONS COLD MILK
SUGAR
CINNAMON

Preheat oven to 450° F.

For filling, combine filling ingredients, except butter, and mix thoroughly. Place in a buttered 10-inch, deep-dish pie plate and dot with butter.

For pinwheels, sift the flour before measuring, then resift it with the salt, baking powder, and sugar. Cut in butter with pastry blender. Adding milk slowly, toss mixture lightly together, using only enough milk to hold ingredients together. Roll out on a floured pastry cloth to only ¼-inch thickness. Sprinkle lightly with sugar and cinnamon. Roll like a jelly roll. Carefully slice with a sharp, thin-bladed knife into 10 equal slices. Place, crowding together, on top of pie filling. Bake for 10 minutes. Reduce to 350° F. and bake for 35 minutes more.

Miriam Warzyniec, Ypsilanti, MI

RHUBARB COBBLER I

Yield: 6 servings

▼▼▼▼▼▼▼▼▼▼▼▼▼▼▼▼▼▼▼▼▼

FILLING:
½ CUP HONEY
⅓ CUP ALL-PURPOSE FLOUR
1 TEASPOON GRATED LEMON PEEL
4 CUPS DICED RHUBARB

TOPPING:
¾ CUP ALL-PURPOSE FLOUR
1 TEASPOON BAKING POWDER
¼ TEASPOON SALT
⅔ CUP SUGAR
1 EGG, BEATEN
¼ CUP MELTED BUTTER

Preheat oven to 350° F.

For filling, combine all filling ingredients and pour into a 9-inch square baking dish.

For topping, sift together flour, baking powder, and salt. Stir in sugar and then egg. Mix until it resembles course crumbs. Sprinkle over rhubarb mixture in the baking dish. Drizzle with butter. Bake for about 40 minutes, or until rhubarb is bubbly and topping is browned.

Maureen Patricia Darby, Lebanon, MO

RHUBARB COBBLER II

Yield: 10 servings

▼▼▼▼▼▼▼▼▼▼▼▼▼▼▼▼▼▼▼▼▼

3 CUPS DICED RHUBARB
2 CUPS SUGAR
1 TEASPOON BUTTER
½ CUP VEGETABLE SHORTENING
1 EGG, BEATEN
1 CUP ALL-PURPOSE FLOUR
PINCH SALT
1 TEASPOON BAKING POWDER
¼ TEASPOON NUTMEG
½ CUP MILK
¼ TEASPOON VANILLA EXTRACT

Preheat oven to 350° F. Arrange rhubarb in a 7½" x 12" greased pan. Top with 1 cup sugar and butter. Cream shortening and remaining sugar. Add egg. Sift flour, salt, baking powder, and nutmeg together. Add alternately with milk and vanilla. Pour over rhubarb. Bake for 50-60 minutes.

Janice Pumphrey, Carmi, IL

RHUBARB-STRAWBERRY PIE

Yield: 6 servings

▼▼▼▼▼▼▼▼▼▼▼▼▼▼▼▼▼▼▼▼▼

¾ CUP SUGAR

¼ CUP ALL-PURPOSE FLOUR

½ TEASPOON GRATED ORANGE RIND

¼ TEASPOON SALT

4 CUPS SLICED RHUBARB

2 CUPS SLICED STRAWBERRIES

2 TABLESPOONS MELTED MARMALADE (ANY KIND)

TWO 9-INCH PIE SHELLS, UNBAKED

2 TABLESPOONS BUTTER

¼ CUP ORANGE LIQUEUR

Preheat oven to 400° F. Mix together sugar, flour, orange rind, and salt. Combine rhubarb and strawberries into sugar mixture. Brush bottom pie shell with marmalade. Place fruit on marmalade. Dot with butter and sprinkle with orange liqueur. Top with crust. Bake for 1 hour.

Georgiann Carroll, Tucson, AZ

RHUBARB-PINEAPPLE CRUMB PIE

Yield: 6 servings

This is my Grandma Dolly's recipe. It is made with my Grandpa Robert's rhubarb, which has been divided and transplanted for over 40 years.

▼▼▼▼▼▼▼▼▼▼▼▼▼▼▼▼▼▼▼▼▼▼

FILLING:

3 CUPS DICED RHUBARB (PREFERABLY YOUNG, RED STALKS)
ONE 8-OUNCE CAN CRUSHED PINEAPPLE, DRAINED
1⅓ CUPS SUGAR
6 TABLESPOONS ALL-PURPOSE FLOUR
½ TEASPOON CINNAMON
ONE 9-INCH PIE SHELL, UNBAKED

TOPPING:

¾ CUP SIFTED ALL-PURPOSE FLOUR
1 CUP SUGAR
⅓ CUP BUTTER, AT ROOM TEMPERATURE

Preheat oven to 425° F.

For filling, combine rhubarb, pineapple, sugar, flour, and cinnamon and place in a pie shell.

For topping, combine all topping ingredients and work with a fork until crumbly and the size of small peas. Spread over pie filling. Bake for about 40 minutes, or until top is golden. Serve warm with vanilla ice cream.

Barbara Muldrew, Garden City, KS

RHUBARB-RAISIN PIE
Yield: 6-8 servings

In our community, rhubarb is commonly called "pie plant." We suggest using golden raisins for a fine color combination with the rhubarb.

▼▼▼▼▼▼▼▼▼▼▼▼▼▼▼▼▼▼▼▼▼▼

PASTRY FOR TWO 9-INCH PIE CRUSTS
3½ CUPS DICED RHUBARB
½ CUP RAISINS
1 CUP SUGAR
¼ TEASPOON CINNAMON
¼ TEASPOON SALT
1 TEASPOON VANILLA
1 EGG, BEATEN
1 TABLESPOON LEMON JUICE
MILK AND SUGAR (OPTIONAL)

Preheat oven to 425° F. Prepare pastry.

Combine rhubarb and raisins. Mix together sugar, cinnamon, salt, vanilla, egg, and lemon juice. Pour over rhubarb mixture, stirring lightly until blended.

Place rhubarb mixture in a pastry-lined 9-inch pie plate. Top with crust, and cut slits in the top for release of steam. Brush the top crust and edges with milk and sprinkle with sugar, if desired. Bake for 10 minutes. Reduce heat to 350° F. and bake approximately 20-30 minutes more.

Donald D. Kaufman, Newton, KS

RHUBARB-ORANGE CREAM PIE

Yield: 8 servings

▼▼▼▼▼▼▼▼▼▼▼▼▼▼▼▼▼▼▼▼

3 EGGS
1¼ CUPS SUGAR
¼ CUP BUTTER OR MARGARINE
3 TABLESPOONS UNDILUTED ORANGE JUICE CONCENTRATE
¼ CUP ALL-PURPOSE FLOUR
¼ TEASPOON SALT
2½ CUPS DICED RHUBARB
⅓ CUP CHOPPED NUTS (ANY KIND, OPTIONAL)
ONE 9-INCH PIE SHELL, UNBAKED

Preheat oven to 375° F.

Separate eggs and beat egg whites. Gradually add ¼ cup sugar, and beat until stiff. Set aside. Add butter and juice to egg yolks and heat. Add remaining sugar, flour, and salt, and beat well. Add rhubarb to egg yolk mixture. Stir well.

Fold reserved meringue into rhubarb mixture and pour into pie shell. Sprinkle nuts on top. Bake on bottom rack for 15 minutes. Reduce heat to 325° F. and bake for 45-50 minutes more.

Rita Hanson, Torrington, WY

CHERRY AND GRAPE PIES

FRESH CHERRY PIE

Yield: 8 servings

▼▼▼▼▼▼▼▼▼▼▼▼▼▼▼▼▼▼▼▼▼▼

1⅓ CUPS SUGAR
⅓ CUP ALL-PURPOSE FLOUR
4 DROPS ALMOND EXTRACT
4 CUPS PITTED CHERRIES
PASTRY FOR TWO 9-INCH PIE CRUSTS
1½ TABLESPOONS BUTTER

Preheat oven to 425° F. Mix together sugar, flour, and almond extract. Mix lightly with cherries. Pour into pastry-lined 9-inch pie pan. Dot with butter. Cover with top crust which has slits cut in it. Seal and flute. Bake for 35-45 minutes, or until crust is nicely browned and juice begins to bubble through slits in crust. Serve warm.

Mrs. Leonard Moeller, So. Elgin, IL

CHEERY CHERRY PIE

Yield: 6-8 servings

I named my pie Cheery Cherry Pie because it always cheers me up when I bake it for my family. I remember picking cherries when I was a little girl, seeing the clear, blue sky through the leaves of the cherry trees and the happy of chatter my three sisters and me—a very "cheery" memory. My two children now help pick cherries, see that same clear, blue sky, and create their own happy chatter.

▼▼▼▼▼▼▼▼▼▼▼▼▼▼▼▼▼▼▼▼▼

CRUST:	FILLING:
2 CUPS ALL-PURPOSE FLOUR	6 CUPS PITTED SOUR CHERRIES
1¼ TEASPOONS SUGAR	½ TEASPOON VANILLA EXTRACT
½ TEASPOON SALT	1½ TABLESPOONS LEMON JUICE
¾ CUP VEGETABLE SHORTENING	1¾ CUPS SUGAR
1¼ TEASPOONS VINEGAR	7 TABLESPOONS QUICK TAPIOCA
1 SMALL EGG	2¼ TABLESPOONS BUTTER
¼ CUP WATER	

For crust, mix flour, sugar, and salt with a fork. Add shortening and mix until crumbly. In a small bowl, beat vinegar, egg, and water. Add to flour mixture, stir, and divide dough in half. Wrap each half in wax paper and chill for 30 minutes. Lightly flour dough on both sides. Roll ⅛ inch thick.

Preheat oven to 450° F. For filling, toss cherries with vanilla, lemon juice, and sugar. Stir in tapioca and let stand for 10 minutes. Line a 12-inch pie pan with half the crust. Pour filling into crust. Dot with butter. Cover with top crust and seal edges by pressing with fork tip, dipped frequently in flour. Cut vents in the shape of a large "C" with scattered cuts around it. Bake for 10 minutes. Reduce heat to 350° F. and bake 40 minutes more.

Mrs. Debbie Snyder, Catawissa, PA

HEARTS AND CHERRIES

Yield: 6 servings

▼▼▼▼▼▼▼▼▼▼▼▼▼▼▼▼▼▼▼▼▼

¾ CUP SUGAR

4 TABLESPOONS ALL-PURPOSE FLOUR

2 TEASPOONS QUICK TAPIOCA

4 CUPS FRESH NORTH STAR CHERRIES, OR 1 QUART
FROZEN NORTH STAR CHERRIES (THAWED AND DRAINED)

½ TEASPOON ALMOND EXTRACT

DOUGH FOR ONE 9-INCH, DOUBLE-CRUST PIE, UNBAKED

SUGAR

Preheat oven to 425° F.

Combine in a small bowl sugar, flour, and tapioca. Stir together. Stir mixture into cherries. Mix well and add almond extract. Mix again with wooden spoon. Pour into pie shell.

For top crust, cut six heart shapes with a cookie cutter and one small circular shape, about 1"-1½" in diameter. Arrange hearts around the center circle. Sprinkle lightly with sugar. Shield outer crust with aluminum foil. Bake at 425° F. for 20 minutes. Reduce heat to 350° F. and continue baking for 45-60 minutes more, or until center is bubbly. Remove foil after the first 30 minutes of baking.

Margaret Felling, Iowa City, IA

FRESH CHERRY-CHOCOLATE CHIP PIE

Yield: 8 servings

▼▼▼▼▼▼▼▼▼▼▼▼▼▼▼▼▼▼▼▼▼▼▼

4 cups pitted, fresh, red North Star cherries
1½ cups sugar
⅓ cup cornstarch
4 drops almond extract
10 drops red food coloring (optional)
1 cup chocolate chips
Pastry for two 9-inch pie crusts
1 tablespoon butter or margarine

Preheat oven to 375° F. In a large bowl, combine cherries, sugar, cornstarch, almond extract, red food coloring, and chocolate chips. Mix together. Fill a pastry-lined 9-inch pie plate with the cherry mixture and top with butter or margarine. Top pie with lattice crust and flute edge. Bake for 25-30 minutes, or until crust is golden.

Tami Bohannan, West Valley, UT

MICROWAVE CHERRY PIE

Yield: 6 servings

▼▼▼▼▼▼▼▼▼▼▼▼▼▼▼▼▼▼▼▼▼▼

¾ CUP SUGAR

2 TABLESPOONS CORNSTARCH

TWO 10-OUNCE CANS RED, TART CHERRIES, PITTED AND UNDRAINED

3 OR 4 DROPS RED FOOD COLORING

½ TEASPOON CINNAMON

¼ TEASPOON NUTMEG

¼ TEASPOON ALMOND EXTRACT

TWO 9-INCH PIE SHELLS, MICROWAVED OR BAKED

Combine sugar and cornstarch in a 1½-quart bowl, stirring well. Drain cherries, reserving ¾ cup juice. Set cherries aside. Stir cherry juice into sugar mixture and add food coloring. Microwave, uncovered, on HIGH for 5-6 minutes, or until mixture is thickened, stirring after every minute.

Stir reserved cherries, cinnamon, nutmeg, and almond extract into sugar mixture. Spoon into pie shell in a microwave-safe pie pan. Cover with top crust. Microwave, uncovered, on HIGH for 2-3 minutes or until heated through. Cool completely before serving.

George N. Melson, Mexico, MO

BEST-EVER CHERRY PIE
Yield: 6-8 servings

▼▼▼▼▼▼▼▼▼▼▼▼▼▼▼▼▼▼▼▼▼▼

FILLING:
¾ CUP SUGAR
3 TABLESPOONS CORNSTARCH
DASH SALT
¾ CUP CHERRY JUICE
2 TABLESPOONS MARGARINE
1 TEASPOON FRESH LEMON JUICE
3 CUPS DRAINED RED, TART NORTH STAR
CHERRIES

CRUST:
1½ CUPS ALL-PURPOSE FLOUR, SIFTED WITH
1 TEASPOON BAKING POWDER
½ TEASPOON SALT
½ CUP PLUS 2 TABLESPOONS CRISCO BUTTER-
FLAVORED SHORTENING
2 EGGS
3 TABLESPOONS WATER
1 TABLESPOON WHITE VINEGAR

For filling, place in a saucepan ¼ cup sugar, cornstarch, and salt. Mix well. Add cherry juice and cook, stirring constantly, until thick and clear. Add the remaining sugar and cook briefly until glossy. Remove from heat, add margarine and lemon juice and stir. Add cherries and set aside.

Preheat oven to 450° F. For crust, mix together flour, baking powder, and salt. Cut shortening into flour mixture. In a separate bowl, beat 1 egg. Add water and vinegar and beat again. Pour egg mixture into flour mixture all at once. Blend with a spoon until all flour is moistened. Form into a ball. Cut three-quarters of the ball for lower crust and one-quarter for top crust. Roll out bottom crust and place it in a 9-inch pie pan. Beat other egg and brush the bottom crust, allowing it to dry. Fill with cherry filling.

Place the top crust on pie, and brush with the remaining beaten egg. Bake at 450° for 15 minutes. Reduce heat to 350° F. and bake for 25-30 minutes more.

Adele M. Anderle, Glen Ellyn, IL

CHERRY COBBLER

Yield: 8 servings

Fresh, frozen, or canned fruits, such as apples, peaches, or blackberries, may also be used for this cobbler. If packed in liquid, drain and use juice as part of the sugar syrup. If not enough juice, always add water to make 2 cups liquid.

▼▼▼▼▼▼▼▼▼▼▼▼▼▼▼▼▼▼▼▼▼▼

½ CUP BUTTER OR MARGARINE
2 CUPS SUGAR
2 CUPS CHERRY JUICE
1 TEASPOON ALMOND EXTRACT
½ CUP VEGETABLE SHORTENING
1½ CUPS SIFTED SELF-RISING FLOUR
⅓ CUP MILK
2 CUPS COOKED AND DRAINED SOUR CHERRIES

Preheat oven to 350° F. Melt butter in a 13" x 9" x 2" baking dish or sheet cake pan.

In a saucepan, heat sugar, cherry juice, and almond extract until sugar dissolves. Cut shortening into flour until particles resemble fine bread crumbs. Add milk. Stir with fork until dough leaves side of bowl. Turn out on lightly floured surface. Knead until smooth. Roll dough into a large rectangle, about ¼ inch thick. Spread cherries evenly over dough. Roll up like a jelly roll. Dampen edge with water and seal. Place in the baking dish with melted butter. Slice dough into about 16 slices, ½ inch thick. Carefully pour sugar syrup around the roll. (This looks like too much liquid, but the crust will absorb it.) Bake for 55-60 minutes.

Ethel B. Lamanca, Roanoke, VA

CHERRY COBBLER WITH ALMONDS

Yield: 8-10 servings

▼▼▼▼▼▼▼▼▼▼▼▼▼▼▼▼▼▼▼▼▼▼

4 CUPS PITTED, FRESH, UNSWEETENED, TART
RED CHERRIES (OR FROZEN AND THAWED)
1 CUP WATER
¾ CUP SUGAR
3 TABLESPOONS QUICK TAPIOCA
1 CUP ALL-PURPOSE FLOUR
2 TABLESPOONS SUGAR
1½ TEASPOONS BAKING POWDER

¼ TEASPOON SALT
¼ CUP BUTTER OR MARGARINE, AT ROOM
TEMPERATURE
¼ CUP FINELY CHOPPED ALMONDS
1 EGG, SLIGHTLY BEATEN
¼ CUP MILK
2 TABLESPOONS BUTTER OR MARGARINE
2 DROPS ALMOND EXTRACT

In a saucepan combine cherries, water, ¾ cup sugar, and tapioca. Let stand while making biscuits.

For biscuits, stir together flour, 2 tablespoons sugar, baking powder, and salt. Cut in ¼ cup butter or margarine until mixture resembles cornmeal. Stir in almonds. Combine egg and milk. Add all at once to the dry ingredients, stirring just to moisten. Knead gently on a well-floured surface 8-10 times. Roll or pat to ½-inch thickness. Cut into 8-10 rounds with a 2-inch biscuit cutter, dipping cutter into flour between cuts. Cover biscuits until ready to use.

Preheat oven to 400° F. Bring cherry mixture to a boil. Cook and stir until slightly thickened and bubbly. Stir in 2 tablespoons butter or margarine and almond extract. Turn hot cherry mixture into a buttered 2-quart casserole. Immediately place the biscuits, overlapping each other a bit, in a circle on top of hot cherries. Bake for 25-30 minutes. Serve warm with ice cream, if desired.

Nina Kay, New York, NY

QUICK CHERRY COBBLER

Yield: 6-8 servings

▼▼▼▼▼▼▼▼▼▼▼▼▼▼▼▼▼▼▼▼

FILLING:

**3 CUPS PITTED FRESH MONTMORENCY OR
NORTH STAR SOUR CHERRIES (OR FROZEN
AND THAWED)
¼ CUP CORNSTARCH
½ CUP SUGAR
4 DROPS ALMOND EXTRACT (OPTIONAL)
2 TABLESPOONS BUTTER**

TOPPING:

**1 CUP ALL-PURPOSE FLOUR
1¼ TEASPOONS BAKING POWDER
2 TEASPOONS SUGAR
3 TABLESPOONS BUTTER
3 TABLESPOONS MILK**

Preheat oven to 425° F.

For filling, stir together cherries, cornstarch, and ½ cup sugar. Cook on low heat until hot, stirring often. Add almond extract and stir. Place in an 8" x 8" baking dish and dot with 2 tablespoons butter.

For topping, use a fork to mix together flour, baking powder, and 2 teaspoons sugar until blended. Cut in 3 tablespoons butter with a fork or pastry blender. Add milk to butter mixture and stir with a fork. Pat between two sheets of floured, wax paper until dough is ¼ inch thick. Transfer dough to top of cherries. Bake for about 30 minutes.

Microwave Options:

Frozen cherries may be thawed in a microwave oven. To save time, the cherry-sugar-cornstarch mixture may also be heated directly in the baking dish in a microwave oven, if the dish is microwave-safe. Simply stir cherries, cornstarch, and sugar together and heat and stir at 2-minute intervals on full power until the dish remains hot to the touch, even after stirring for 6-8 minutes.

Mary Jo Kearns, Valley Falls, KS

CHERRY-RASPBERRY PIE
Yield: 6-8 servings

▼▼▼▼▼▼▼▼▼▼▼▼▼▼▼▼▼▼▼▼▼▼▼

4 TABLESPOONS CORNSTARCH
1 CUP SUGAR
3 CUPS FRESH SOUR CHERRIES (OR FROZEN AND THAWED)
1 CUP FRESH RED RASPBERRIES (OR FROZEN AND THAWED)
PASTRY FOR TWO 9-INCH PIE CRUSTS
1 TABLESPOON BUTTER
1 TABLESPOON SUGAR

Preheat oven to 425° F. Combine cornstarch and sugar. Mix with cherries, stirring until well blended. Fold in raspberries. Pour into a pastry-lined 9-inch pie dish. Dot with butter. Cover with lattice-top pastry. Sprinkle with sugar. Bake for about 50 minutes, or until filling is bubbly and crust is browned.

Marilyn Farrell, Independence, MO

CHERRY-BERRY PIE

Yield: 8 servings

▼▼▼▼▼▼▼▼▼▼▼▼▼▼▼▼▼▼▼▼▼

2 CUPS PITTED CHERRIES
2 CUPS BLACKBERRIES
¾ CUP SUGAR
3 TABLESPOONS MINUTE TAPIOCA
TWO 9-INCH PIE SHELLS, UNBAKED

Preheat oven to 350° F. Mix fruits, sugar, and tapioca. Pour into pie shell, topping with second pie crust. Bake for 1 hour.

Variation: Cook cherries on top of stove with ¾ cup sugar, 2½ tablespoons cornstarch, ½ teaspoon salt, and ⅔ cup water. Cook until very thick. Stir in blackberries and cool. Pour into baked pie crust and top with cream. Chill for 1-2 hours.

Sheila Delzer, Redgranite, WI

CHERRY-BLUEBERRY PIE

Yield: 8 servings

▼▼▼▼▼▼▼▼▼▼▼▼▼▼▼▼▼▼▼▼▼

CRUST:

2/3 CUP VEGETABLE SHORTENING
2 TABLESPOONS COLD BUTTER
2 CUPS ALL-PURPOSE FLOUR
1 TEASPOON SALT
4 TABLESPOONS ICE WATER
1 TABLESPOON WHITE VINEGAR
1 TEASPOON-1 TABLESPOON ADDITIONAL ICE
WATER, IF NEEDED

FILLING:

3 CUPS PITTED FRESH SOUR CHERRIES
1-2 CUPS FRESH BLUEBERRIES
1/8 TEASPOON ALMOND EXTRACT
1 CUP SUGAR
2½ TABLESPOONS QUICK TAPIOCA

Preheat oven to 450° F.

For crust, cut shortening and butter into flour and salt mixture until grainy consistency. Sprinkle dough with a mixture of 4 tablespoons ice water and vinegar. Mix with fork until dough gathers into a tidy ball. Divide in half. Roll out half of the dough for bottom crust for a 10-inch pie plate. Reserve other half for lattice top.

For filling, combine all ingredients and mix. Pour into bottom crust. Make a lattice top. Bake for 10 minutes. Reduce heat to 350° F. and bake for 50-60 minutes more, or until fruit bubbles and crust is golden brown. Serve warm with vanilla or cinnamon ice cream.

Maribeth Deavers, Sunbury, OH

MOM'S GRAPE PIE

Yield: 4 - 6 servings

*M*y mom, who gave me this recipe, was a great cook and always could put a recipe together by just thinking about it. She could taste something, somewhere once, and make it from scratch.

▼▼▼▼▼▼▼▼▼▼▼▼▼▼▼▼▼▼▼▼

CRUST:
FLOUR
1 CUP WHOLE WHEAT PASTRY FLOUR
1 CUP RICE FLOUR
½ TEASPOON SALT
4 TABLESPOONS MARGARINE OR BUTTER
2 TABLESPOONS VEGETABLE OIL
2 TABLESPOONS ICE WATER

FILLING:
4 CUPS RED GRAPES (WASHED WELL)
6 TABLESPOONS HONEY
GRATED RIND OF 1 LEMON
1½ TABLESPOONS LEMON JUICE
3 TABLESPOONS QUICK TAPIOCA
1 TABLESPOON MARGARINE OR BUTTER

Preheat oven to 400° F.

For crust, sprinkle a 9-inch pie pan with flour. Mix whole wheat pastry flour and rice flour with salt in a bowl and cut in margarine with a knife. Add oil gradually. Add ice water. Knead briefly to blend everything together. Press dough into pie pan, saving some dough for lattice top. Flute edges. Bake for 10-12 minutes.

Peel grapes. Bring pulp to a boil and simmer for 5 minutes. Strain to remove seeds. In a blender, puree pulp, skins, honey, lemon rind, lemon juice, and tapioca. Pour into pie crust. Cut margarine or butter into small bits and dot surface. Roll out remaining pastry dough and cut into strips ½ inch wide. Lay strips across filling. Reduce heat to 350° F. and bake for 15 minutes. Reduce heat again to 325° F. and bake 30 minutes more, or until filling is boiling and tapioca is cooked. Cool. Serve warm or cold.

Gertrude Prince, Laurelton Queens, NY

TIGGER'S GRAPE PIE

Yield: 6 servings

This pie was first made by my grandmother during the trying times of the Depression years. It came to light again nearly fifty years later when my mother had a bumper crop of grapes and a chance to remember her childhood. The pie has become such a family favorite that it is now used by third- and fourth-generation pie makers.

▼▼▼▼▼▼▼▼▼▼▼▼▼▼▼▼▼▼▼▼▼▼

2 CUPS SEEDLESS, RED GRAPES
1-1½ CUPS WATER
2 TABLESPOONS CORNSTARCH
1 TABLESPOON ALL-PURPOSE FLOUR
½ CUP SUGAR
1 TABLESPOON BUTTER
1 TABLESPOON VANILLA EXTRACT
TWO 8-INCH PIE SHELLS, UNBAKED

Preheat oven to 375° F.

Mix together in a saucepan, grapes, water, cornstarch, flour, and sugar. Cook until mixture begins to thicken, stirring often. Add butter and vanilla. Continue cooking until mixture comes to a boil. Taste and add more sugar and vanilla, if desired. (Be careful not to break the grapes, they should be left whole.)

Pour grape mixture into pie shell and top with vented crust. Bake for 45-50 minutes, or until crust is golden.

June Krell, Haven, KS

GREAT GRAPE PIE

Yield: 6 servings

I created this crust recipe with safflower oil as a healthier alternative to the traditional lard crust.

▼▼▼▼▼▼▼▼▼▼▼▼▼▼▼▼▼▼▼▼

CRUST:

2⅔ CUPS ALL-PURPOSE FLOUR

1 TEASPOON SALT

¾ CUP SAFFLOWER OIL

4-5 TABLESPOONS COLD WATER

FILLING:

4 CUPS GRAPES (CONCORD, NIAGARA, OR CATAWBA)

⅔ CUP SUGAR

⅓ CUP ALL-PURPOSE FLOUR

⅛ TEASPOON SALT

⅛ TEASPOON NUTMEG

1 TABLESPOON LEMON JUICE

BUTTER

Preheat oven to 450° F.

For crust, mix flour and salt. Add oil and mix with pastry blender. Stir in water. Dough rolls out easier if put between two sheets of wax paper. Place dough in a 9-inch pie pan.

For filling, peel grapes, but save skins. Heat grapes to a boil. Press through a colander. Mix skins back in. Mix together dry ingredients. Sprinkle half of flour mixture on bottom of crust. Mix remaining flour mixture with pulp and skins. Stir in lemon juice and pour mixture in crust. Dot with butter. Bake for 10 minutes. Reduce heat to 350° F. and bake 25-30 minutes more.

Debi Snyder, W. Jefferson, OH

STRAWBERRY PIES

FRESH STRAWBERRY PIE I

Yield: 6 servings

This recipe is one I made up. It's so simple and everyone begs for the recipe, so I finally measured it out so you can share it. I don't always measure when I cook. My husband calls me "old-sling-it-together." I'm a "young" 73-year-old and love to cook.

▼▼▼▼▼▼▼▼▼▼▼▼▼▼▼▼▼▼▼▼▼

1 QUART STRAWBERRIES, HULLED
1 CUP SUGAR
3 TABLESPOONS CORNSTARCH
ONE **8-** OR **9-**INCH PIE SHELL, BAKED
1 CUP WHIPPED CREAM OR OTHER TOPPING

Place strawberries in a double boiler and mash thoroughly. Heat to boiling point. Add sugar combined with cornstarch. Stir constantly until smooth and clear. (The secret is not to overcook.) Cool. Pour into pie shell. Place in the refrigerator to chill. Serve with whipped cream.

Mrs. Lilias Wint, Independence, KS

FRESH STRAWBERRY PIE II

Yield: 6 servings

▼▼▼▼▼▼▼▼▼▼▼▼▼▼▼▼▼▼▼▼▼▼

CRUST:

½ CUP BUTTER, AT ROOM TEMPERATURE
1 CUP ALL-PURPOSE FLOUR
¼ CUP LIGHT BROWN SUGAR
⅓ CUP CHOPPED PECANS

FILLING:

1 CUP WHOLE STRAWBERRIES, HULLED
¾ CUP WATER
1 CUP GRANULATED SUGAR
2½ TABLESPOONS CORNSTARCH
1½ QUARTS FRESH STRAWBERRIES, HULLED AND SLICED
WHIPPED CREAM

Preheat oven to 375° F.

For crust, blend butter, flour, and brown sugar until crumbs form. Stir in pecans. Press mixture into a 9-inch pie plate. Bake for 12-15 minutes or until golden brown.

For filling, crush 1 cup whole strawberries in a small saucepan. Add water, granulated sugar, and cornstarch. Cook, stirring until mixture thickens. Cool.

Arrange remaining sliced berries in pie shell. Pour cooled, cooked berry glaze over the fresh berries. Chill until serving time. Top with whipped cream.

Barbara Eicher, Loogootee, IN

STRAWBERRY PIE
Yield: 6-8 servings

▼▼▼▼▼▼▼▼▼▼▼▼▼▼▼▼▼▼▼▼▼

1 QUART STRAWBERRIES, HULLED
1 CUP SUGAR
3 TABLESPOONS CORNSTARCH
¾ CUP WATER
1 TABLESPOON LEMON JUICE
ONE 9-INCH PIE SHELL, BAKED AND COOLED

In a saucepan, crush 1½ cups strawberries and combine with sugar, cornstarch, and water. Cook until thickened. Cool. Add lemon juice. Slice remaining berries in pie shell and pour cooked mixture over berries. Chill for 1-2 hours. Serve with whipped cream.

Cathy White, Montrose, CO

STRAWBERRY GLACÉ PIE

Yield: 6-8 servings

▼▼▼▼▼▼▼▼▼▼▼▼▼▼▼▼▼▼▼▼▼▼

1 QUART FRESH STRAWBERRIES, HULLED
ONE 8-INCH PIE SHELL, BAKED OR MICROWAVED*
⅓ CUP SUGAR
1½ TABLESPOONS CORNSTARCH
1 PINT FROZEN STRAWBERRIES, SWEETENED AND THAWED
1 TABLESPOON LEMON JUICE

Wash and dry strawberries. Place in pie shell. In a bowl, combine sugar and cornstarch. Stir in thawed strawberries. Microwave on HIGH for 4-8 minutes or until thickened and clear, stirring every 2 minutes. Stir in lemon juice. Cool. Spoon mixture over fresh berries. Refrigerate.

*Pie crust can be microwaved on HIGH for 4-5 minutes.

Anne L. Wamsley, Eaton Rapids, MI

STRAWBERRY CRUMBLE

Yield: 6 servings

▼▼▼▼▼▼▼▼▼▼▼▼▼▼▼▼▼▼

FILLING:

1 POUND FIRM, RIPE STRAWBERRIES

SUGAR FOR SPRINKLING

TOPPING:

6 OUNCES SELF-RISING FLOUR

½ TEASPOON CINNAMON

5 TABLESPOONS BUTTER, AT ROOM TEMPERATURE

¾ CUP BROWN SUGAR

GRATED ZEST OF 1 ORANGE

Preheat oven to 350° F.

For filling, wash and hull strawberries. Slice the berries, only if they are very large. Drain and put into a 9-inch pie dish, powdering with a little sugar in between layers.

For topping, mix flour and cinnamon. Blend in butter and stir in brown sugar and orange zest. Sprinkle topping mixture over fruit. *Do not* press down. Bake for 35 minutes.

Maria T. Boone, La Plata, MD

STRAWBERRY-RHUBARB CRUMB PIE

Yield: 6 servings

▼▼▼▼▼▼▼▼▼▼▼▼▼▼▼▼▼▼▼▼▼▼▼

FILLING:
3 CUPS DICED RHUBARB
3 CUPS STRAWBERRIES, HULLED AND HALVED
1 CUP SUGAR
1½ TABLESPOONS LEMON JUICE
1½ TABLESPOONS MARGARINE, AT ROOM TEMPERATURE
5 TABLESPOONS CORNSTARCH
ONE 10-INCH DEEP-DISH, PIE SHELL BAKED

TOPPING:
¾ CUP ALL-PURPOSE FLOUR
⅓ CUP GRANULATED SUGAR
½ CUP LIGHT BROWN SUGAR
4 TABLESPOONS COLD MARGARINE

Preheat oven to 375° F.

For filling, mix all filling ingredients and cook until rhubarb and strawberries are soft and mixture is thickened.

For topping, combine all ingredients and mix until crumbly. Pour filling into pie shell and top with crumbs. Bake for 15-20 minutes, or until topping is light brown.

Luella C. Brown, Allentown, PA

4TH-OF-JULY PIE

Yield: 8 servings

▼▼▼▼▼▼▼▼▼▼▼▼▼▼▼▼▼▼▼▼

1 PACKAGE REFRIGERATED SUGAR-COOKIE DOUGH, OR 1 GRAHAM-CRACKER CRUST

½ CUP SUGAR

3 TABLESPOONS CORNSTARCH

1½ CUPS ORANGE JUICE

¼ CUP LEMON JUICE

3 CUPS FRESH STRAWBERRIES, HULLED AND HALVED

3 CUPS FRESH BLUEBERRIES

Preheat oven to 400° F.

Press cookie dough into 9-inch pie plate to form crust. Bake for approximately 8 minutes, or until edge is browned. Cool. (Or, have ready graham-cracker crust.)

In a saucepan, mix sugar and cornstarch. Gradually stir in orange juice until smooth. Stirring constantly, bring to a boil on medium heat and boil for 1 minute. Remove from heat. Stir in lemon juice. Cool completely.

Mix half of the orange juice mixture with strawberries, other half of mixture with blueberries. Spoon strawberry mixture into outside edge of pie crust and put blueberry mixture into center. Chill for 4 hours or more. Serve with a dollop of whipped cream.

Karen Kaler, Newark, DE

Blueberry, Blackberry, Raspberry, and Other Berry Pies

▼▼

GRANDMA FOX'S GLAZED BLUEBERRY PIE

Yield: 6 servings

▼▼▼▼▼▼▼▼▼▼▼▼▼▼▼▼▼▼▼

CRUST:

2 CUPS ALL-PURPOSE FLOUR
1 TEASPOON SALT
1 CUP CRISCO
7 TABLESPOONS ICE WATER
FLOUR FOR DUSTING SURFACE

FILLING:

3 CUPS MEDIUM TO LARGE, FRESH BLUEBERRIES

¾ CUP WATER
½ CUP SUGAR
1 TABLESPOON CORNSTARCH
½ TEASPOON LEMON JUICE
DASH SALT
¼ PINT HEAVY WHIPPING CREAM
1 HEAPING TEASPOON CONFECTIONERS' SUGAR
1 TEASPOON VANILLA EXTRACT

Preheat oven to 350° F.

For crust, mix together all crust ingredients, using enough flour for a nonsticky dough. Roll out flat and place in a 9-inch pie pan. Prick the dough all over with a fork and bake for approximately 20 minutes or until golden. Cool.

For filling, take ¾ cup drained blueberries and place in a saucepan. Add ½ cup water and sugar and bring to a boil. Reduce heat and simmer until berries are soft. Put this mixture through a food mill—juice and all—or place in a blender, then strain out blueberry skins. Place mixture back in saucepan. Dissolve cornstarch in remaining ¼ cup cold water. Add cornstarch mixture to the juices in the saucepan. Bring to a boil, stirring constantly for 4 minutes or until thick. Cool slightly, then add lemon juice and salt.

Put remaining whole, drained berries into pie shell and add glaze. Chill before serving. Whip cream over a bowl filled with ice, and add confectioners' sugar and vanilla. Top chilled pie with whipped cream mixture just before serving.

Denise M. Fox, Wilton, NH

SHORTY'S FRESH BLUEBERRY PIE

Yield: 6 servings

Blueberry pies need a little salt with the berries to give them savor. A dash of black pepper also helps. When very juicy, use Minute Tapioca instead of flour. This makes the filling solid when cold and gives a better flavor than flour. You can also thinly slice a banana and put on bottom crust for added flavor.

▼▼▼▼▼▼▼▼▼▼▼▼▼▼▼▼▼▼▼▼▼

PASTRY FOR TWO 9-INCH PIE CRUSTS

5 CUPS FRESH BLUEBERRIES

1 CUP SUGAR

¼ CUP ALL-PURPOSE FLOUR, OR 2 TABLESPOONS MINUTE TAPIOCA

½ TEASPOON FINELY GRATED LEMON PEEL

DASH SALT

2 TEASPOONS LEMON JUICE

1½ TABLESPOONS BUTTER

Preheat oven to 375° F.

Prepare and roll out pastry. Line a 9-inch pie pan with half the pastry and trim pastry to edge of pie pan.

In a mixing bowl, combine blueberries, sugar, flour, lemon peel, and salt. Pour blueberry mixture into pastry-lined pie pan. Drizzle with lemon juice and dot with butter. Cut slits in top crust and place on top of filling. Seal and flute edge. To prevent over browning, cover edge of pie with aluminum foil. Bake for 20 minutes. Remove foil and bake for 20-25 minutes more, or until crust is golden. Cool pie on cake rack before serving.

George N. Melson, Mexico, MO

FRESH BLUEBERRY PIE I

Yield: 8 servings

▼▼▼▼▼▼▼▼▼▼▼▼▼▼▼▼▼▼▼▼▼▼

4 CUPS BLUEBERRIES

1½ CUPS SUGAR

2 TABLESPOONS ALL-PURPOSE FLOUR

2 TABLESPOONS CORNSTARCH

ONE 9-INCH DEEP-DISH PIE SHELL, UNBAKED

8 OUNCES CREAM CHEESE, AT ROOM TEMPERATURE

2 EGGS

1 TEASPOON VANILLA EXTRACT

½ CUP HEAVY CREAM

Preheat oven to 450° F.

In a bowl, mix blueberries, 1 cup sugar, flour, and cornstarch. Mash some berries to make juice so the dry ingredients can dissolve. Pour into pie shell and bake for 20 minutes.

Beat together cream cheese, eggs, remaining sugar, vanilla, and cream. Pour onto berries. Reduce heat to 350° F. and bake for 45 minutes more. Cool and serve with whipped cream, if desired.

Peg Schultz, Coudersport, PA

FRESH BLUEBERRY PIE II

Yield: 6 servings

▼▼▼▼▼▼▼▼▼▼▼▼▼▼▼▼▼▼▼▼▼

FILLING:

½ CUP GRANULATED SUGAR

⅓ CUP ALL-PURPOSE FLOUR

½ TEASPOON CINNAMON

4½ CUPS FRESH BLUEBERRIES

ONE 9-INCH PIE SHELL, UNBAKED

1 TABLESPOON LEMON JUICE

TOPPING:

1 CUP ALL-PURPOSE FLOUR

½ CUP FIRMLY PACKED BROWN SUGAR

½ CUP BUTTER

Preheat oven to 425° F.

For filling, combine granulated sugar, flour, cinnamon, and blueberries, mixing well. Put blueberry mixture into pie shell. Sprinkle with lemon juice.

For topping, combine flour and brown sugar and cut in butter until mixture resembles coarse meal. Spread topping over blueberry mixture. Bake for 30 minutes. Cover with aluminum foil and bake for 20 minutes more.

George N. Melson, Mexico, MO

SNOW-TOPPED BLUEBERRY CHEESE TORTE

Yield: 8-10 servings

▼▼▼▼▼▼▼▼▼▼▼▼▼▼▼▼▼▼▼▼▼▼

½ CUP BUTTER, AT ROOM TEMPERATURE
⅓ CUP SUGAR
¼ TEASPOON VANILLA EXTRACT
1 CUP UNBLEACHED ALL-PURPOSE FLOUR
8 OUNCES CREAM CHEESE, AT ROOM TEMPERATURE
¼ CUP SUGAR
1 EGG
½ TEASPOON VANILLA EXTRACT
1 PINT BLUEBERRIES
3-4 TABLESPOONS CONFECTIONERS' SUGAR

Preheat oven to 450° F.

Cream butter, sugar, and vanilla until well blended. Add flour and mix thoroughly. Pat onto the bottom and sides of an ungreased, 8-inch springform pan.

Cream the cream cheese and sugar until smooth. Add egg and vanilla and mix until well blended. Spoon onto crust and spread evenly. Top crust and filling with blueberries. Bake for 10 minutes. Reduce heat to 400° F. and continue baking for 25 minutes more, or until crust begins to brown. When cool, sift confectioners' sugar on top for a beautiful effect.

Maureen Gaines, Mohegan Lake, NY

BLUEBERRY CREAM PIE

Yield: 8 servings

▼▼▼▼▼▼▼▼▼▼▼▼▼▼▼▼▼▼▼▼▼

4 OUNCES CREAM CHEESE, AT ROOM TEMPERATURE

½ CUP CONFECTIONERS' SUGAR

½ TEASPOON VANILLA EXTRACT

1 CUP WHIPPING CREAM

ONE 9-INCH PIE SHELL, BAKED

4 CUPS FRESH BLUEBERRIES

¾ CUP WATER

1 TABLESPOON BUTTER

1 CUP GRANULATED SUGAR

½ TEASPOON CINNAMON

3 TABLESPOONS CORNSTARCH

PINCH SALT

1 TABLESPOON FRESHLY SQUEEZED LEMON JUICE

WHIPPED CREAM

Cream together softened cream cheese, confectioners' sugar, and vanilla. Whip cream and fold into cream cheese mixture. Spread into pie shell. Refrigerate.

Bring to a boil in a small saucepan, 1 cup blueberries and water. Simmer for 4 minutes, stirring constantly. Add butter and stir. Mix together granulated sugar, cornstarch, cinnamon, and salt, and add to hot blueberry mixture. Cook on low heat, stirring constantly until thick and clear. Remove from heat and add lemon juice.

Pour remaining blueberries over chilled cream cheese mixture in pie shell. Pour and spread hot blueberry mixture over fresh berries. Refrigerate. Serve with whipped cream.

Sarah Stackhouse, Bluff Point, NY

BLUEBERRY SOUR CREAM PIE

Yield: 6 servings

▼▼▼▼▼▼▼▼▼▼▼▼▼▼▼▼▼▼▼

FILLING:

1 CUP SOUR CREAM

2 TABLESPOONS ALL-PURPOSE FLOUR

¾ CUP SUGAR

1 TEASPOON VANILLA EXTRACT

¼ TEASPOON SALT

1 EGG, BEATEN

2 CUPS (OR MORE) FRESH BLUEBERRIES (OR FROZEN AND THAWED)

ONE 9-INCH PIE SHELL, UNBAKED

TOPPING:

3 TABLESPOONS ALL-PURPOSE FLOUR

3 TABLESPOONS BUTTER

3 TABLESPOONS CHOPPED PECANS

2 TABLESPOONS SUGAR

Preheat oven to 400° F.

For filling, combine first six ingredients and beat for 5 minutes. Fold in blueberries. Pour into pie shell. Bake for 25 minutes.

For topping, combine all topping ingredients and sprinkle on top of pie. Bake for 10 minutes more. Chill before serving.

Mrs. Betty Redding, Louisville, KY

BLUEBERRY COBBLER I
Yield: 6 servings

▼▼▼▼▼▼▼▼▼▼▼▼▼▼▼▼▼▼▼▼▼

FILLING:

½ CUP SUGAR

¼ CUP ALL-PURPOSE FLOUR

¼ TEASPOON CINNAMON

¼ TEASPOON NUTMEG

4½ CUPS FRESH BLUEBERRIES

1 TABLESPOON LEMON JUICE

3 TABLESPOONS MELTED MARGARINE

CRUST:

1½ CUPS ALL-PURPOSE FLOUR

¼ TEASPOON SALT

½ CUP VEGETABLE SHORTENING

ICE WATER

Preheat oven to 350° F.

For filling, mix all filling ingredients and let stand while preparing crust.

For crust, combine crust ingredients, except water, and cut in shortening. Sprinkle ice water on dry mixture, stirring with fork until ingredients are moistened. Roll three-quarters of pastry to ⅛-inch thickness. Fit into an 8-inch square pan.

Pour reserved filling ingredients into crust. Roll remaining pastry to ¼ inch thickness on a lightly floured surface. Cut into ½-inch strips. Arrange in lattice fashion over blueberries. Bake for 45-60 minutes, or until crust is golden.

Virginia B. Legg, Summersville, WV

BLUEBERRY COBBLER II

Yield: 6 servings

My mother and I created this recipe by combining a basic white cake recipe and a blueberry pie filling recipe. I am 14 years old and enrolled in our local 4-H Club. I won a county-wide contest and I was a "final" in the State.

▼▼▼▼▼▼▼▼▼▼▼▼▼▼▼▼▼▼▼▼▼

FILLING:

3 CUPS BLUEBERRIES
⅓ CUP SUGAR
¾ CUP WATER
¼ TEASPOON CINNAMON
2 TABLESPOONS CORNSTARCH
1 TABLESPOON MARGARINE

TOPPING:

⅓ CUP SUGAR
¼ CUP VEGETABLE SHORTENING
1 EGG
2½ TEASPOONS BAKING POWDER
½ CUP MILK
1 TEASPOON VANILLA EXTRACT
½ CUP ROLLED OATS
¾ CUP ALL-PURPOSE FLOUR
1 TABLESPOON WHEAT GERM

For filling, mix blueberries, sugar, water, cinnamon, cornstarch, and margarine in a 1½-quart saucepan. Mix and bring to a boil, stirring occasionally. Boil for 4 minutes. Remove from heat and pour into a 2-quart baking dish or an 8" x 8" pan.

Preheat oven to 350° F.

For topping, cream sugar and shortening together. Add egg, stirring with a whisk until smooth. Run rolled oats through a blender, and add them, along with the remaining ingredients, except wheat germ, and mix well. Spread on top of the filling. Sprinkle wheat germ on top. Bake for 30 minutes.

Lisa Childs, Wellsville, NY

BLACKBERRY PIE
Yield: 6-8 servings

▼▼▼▼▼▼▼▼▼▼▼▼▼▼▼▼▼▼▼▼▼▼

¾ CUP SUGAR
2½ TABLESPOONS CORNSTARCH
4 CUPS BLACKBERRIES
TWO 9-INCH PIE SHELLS, UNBAKED
1 TABLESPOON BUTTER

Preheat oven to 425° F. Mix sugar and cornstarch together. Pour over blackberries and stir gently until blueberries are coated with mixture. Pour into pie shell and dot with butter. Add top crust. Bake for 35-40 minutes.

Agnes Kever, Bonnots Mill, MO

CREAMY BLACKBERRY PIE

Yield: 6 servings

▼▼▼▼▼▼▼▼▼▼▼▼▼▼▼▼▼▼▼▼

3 CUPS FRESH BLACKBERRIES
ONE 9-INCH PIE SHELL, UNBAKED
1½ CUPS SUGAR
⅓ CUP ALL-PURPOSE FLOUR
2 EGGS, BEATEN
½ CUP LOW-FAT PLAIN YOGURT
½ CUP ALL-PURPOSE FLOUR
¼ CUP MARGARINE

Preheat oven to 350° F.

Place blackberries in pie shell. Combine 1 cup sugar and ⅓ cup flour. Add eggs and yogurt and spoon over blackberries.

Combine remaining sugar and ½ cup flour. Cut in margarine until mixture resembles coarse crumbs. Sprinkle over blackberry mixture. Bake for 55 minutes or until lightly browned. This recipe also works without the crust.

Elizabeth Arthurs, Mooresville, NC

BLACKBERRY PINWHEELS COBBLER

Yield: 10-12 servings

▼▼▼▼▼▼▼▼▼▼▼▼▼▼▼▼▼▼▼▼▼

2 CUPS SUGAR
2 CUPS WATER
½ CUP BUTTER OR MARGARINE
½ CUP VEGETABLE SHORTENING
1½ CUPS SELF-RISING FLOUR
⅓ CUP MILK
3-4 CUPS FRESH BLACKBERRIES
1 TEASPOON CINNAMON

Preheat oven to 350° F. Place butter or margarine in a 13" x 9" x 2" pan and melt in the oven. Set aside. Combine sugar and water in a saucepan and stir well. Cook until sugar dissolves. Set aside.

Cut shortening into flour until mixture resembles coarse meal. Add milk and stir until ingredients are moistened. Turn out on floured surface and knead lightly four or five times. Roll dough into a 12" x 9" rectangle. Spread blackberries over dough. Sprinkle with cinnamon. Roll up (jellyroll fashion) beginning with long side. Cut into twelve 1-inch slices and place in buttered baking pan. Pour syrup around slices. Bake for 55-60 minutes or until golden brown on top. Serve.

Alternate: Can be baked in a microwave oven. Use appropriate baking ware and adjust time according to size of microwave oven — approximately 25 minutes in a small oven.

Jeannette Haubold, Marston, MO

EASY BLACKBERRY COBBLER

Yield: 4-6 servings

▼▼▼▼▼▼▼▼▼▼▼▼▼▼▼▼▼▼▼▼

FILLING:

1 CUP SUGAR

1½ TABLESPOONS CORNSTARCH

1 CUP WATER

2 PINTS DRAINED BLACKBERRIES, FRESH OR FROZEN AND THAWED

1 TEASPOON ALMOND EXTRACT

1 TEASPOON CINNAMON

1 TEASPOON NUTMEG

CRUST:

3 TABLESPOONS VEGETABLE OIL

1 CUP SELF-RISING FLOUR

½-¾ CUPS MILK

½ CUP SUGAR

½ TEASPOON LEMON EXTRACT

1 TEASPOON NUTMEG

Preheat oven to 400° F.

For filling, in saucepan, mix 1 cup sugar and cornstarch. Whisk in water. Boil for 1 minute, or until mixture is clear. Stir in blackberries and remaining filling ingredients. Pour into a 1½-quart greased baking dish.

For crust, mix together all the crust ingredients. Pour over the filling. Bake for 25-30 minutes.

Mr. and Mrs. Craig McFadden, Owensboro, KY

THE GODS' RASPBERRY PIE

Yield: 6 servings

I have made lots of "mean" fruit pies during my lifetime, but all my relatives agree that this pie is the absolute best pie in the world. The fruit is the pie! — it sparkles! If you use canned or frozen berries for the cooked mixture, use berry juice (up to ½ cup) instead of the ½ cup water.

▼▼▼▼▼▼▼▼▼▼▼▼▼▼▼▼▼▼▼▼▼▼

CRUST:
1 CUP ALL-PURPOSE FLOUR
⅓ TEASPOON SALT
⅓ CUP CRISCO
3 TABLESPOONS WATER

FILLING:
3 TABLESPOONS CORNSTARCH

½ CUP WATER
2 CUPS RED RASPBERRIES (OR CANNED, OR FROZEN AND THAWED)
¾ CUP SUGAR
3 TABLESPOONS LEMON JUICE
2 CUPS FRESH WHOLE RED RASPBERRIES
WHIPPED CREAM

Preheat oven to 425° F. Make the crust by cutting the Crisco into the flour and salt until the mixture resembles cornmeal. Quickly stir in the water, roll out dough, and place in 9-inch pie pan. Prick with a fork. Bake for 8 minutes or until light brown.

For filling, dissolve cornstarch in ¼ cup water. Mix together 2 cups raspberries, the remaining water or berry juice, sugar, and lemon juice. Bring mixture to a boil. Mix ¼ of the hot berries with the cornstarch and water, stir, and return thickened berries to the hot berry mixture. Cook for 1 minute, and then chill.

At serving time, put 2 cups remaining whole, uncooked raspberries into the baked crust. Pour chilled filling over berries and top with whipped cream.

Mrs. Don H. Lienemann, Papillion, NE

RASPBERRY CUSTARD PIE

Yield: 8 servings

▼▼▼▼▼▼▼▼▼▼▼▼▼▼▼▼▼▼▼▼▼

3 TABLESPOONS ALL-PURPOSE FLOUR

¼ TEASPOON CINNAMON

1½ CUPS SUGAR

3 EGGS, WELL BEATEN

3 CUPS RED RASPBERRIES

PASTRY FOR ONE 9-INCH PIE CRUST

1½ TABLESPOONS BUTTER

Preheat oven to 425° F.

Blend flour, cinnamon, and sugar. Add eggs and blend. Pour over raspberries in a pastry-lined 9-inch pie pan. Slice butter over top. Bake for 10 minutes. Reduce heat to 350° F. and continue baking for 30 minutes more. Several times during the first half of the baking period, cut gently into the lightly browning surface with a large spoon to allow the uncooked custard to flow over the top and prevent too dark a crust from forming.

Mrs. Roy Bohnhoff, Plymouth, WI

RASPBERRY COBBLER

Yield: 8-9 servings

▼▼▼▼▼▼▼▼▼▼▼▼▼▼▼▼▼▼▼▼▼▼▼

4 CUPS FRESH RASPBERRIES
1 STICK MARGARINE, AT ROOM TEMPERATURE
1½ CUPS SUGAR
½ CUP MILK
1 CUP ALL-PURPOSE FLOUR
2 TEASPOONS BAKING POWDER
½ TEASPOON SALT
1 TEASPOON VANILLA EXTRACT
½ CUP WATER

Preheat oven to 350° F.

Line an 8-inch or 9-inch square baking dish with raspberries.

Make batter by mixing margarine, ½ cup sugar, milk, flour, baking powder, salt, and vanilla. Pour batter over fruit and spread evenly. Mix remaining sugar and water. Pour over batter. Bake for 1 hour. Serve warm with cream, ice cream, or whipped cream.

Kay Hendricks, Libertyville, IL

BLACK RASPBERRY CREAM PIE

Yield: 6 servings

▼▼▼▼▼▼▼▼▼▼▼▼▼▼▼▼▼▼▼▼▼▼

2 cups fresh black raspberries (or frozen and thawed)
One 9-inch pie shell, unbaked
¾ cup sugar
4 tablespoons all-purpose flour
1¼ cups cream
1 teaspoon vanilla extract

Preheat oven to 350° F. Sprinkle raspberries in pie shell. Combine sugar and flour and pour over raspberries. Combine cream and vanilla and pour over raspberry mixture. Bake for 1 hour, or until the center is set.

Vera A. Witmer, Goshen, IN

GOOSEBERRY PIE

Yield: 6 servings

▼▼▼▼▼▼▼▼▼▼▼▼▼▼▼▼▼▼▼▼▼

2 CUPS GOOSEBERRIES
2 TABLESPOONS ALL-PURPOSE FLOUR
1 CUP GRANULATED SUGAR
PINCH SALT
TWO 8-INCH PIE SHELLS, UNBAKED
¾ CUP BROWN SUGAR
SEVERAL SLICES MARGARINE

Preheat oven to 350° F. Mix together gooseberries, flour, granulated sugar, and salt. Put this mixture in a pie shell in an 8-inch pie pan. Sprinkle brown sugar over gooseberries and dot with margarine. Put on top crust and seal edge. Bake for approximately 1 hour.

Helen Ellsworth, Tarkio, MO

FRENCH GOOSEBERRY PIE

Yield: 6 servings

▼▼▼▼▼▼▼▼▼▼▼▼▼▼▼▼▼▼▼▼▼

2 CUPS GOOSEBERRIES
2 TABLESPOONS ALL-PURPOSE FLOUR
1 EGG
1 CUP GRANULATED SUGAR
1 TEASPOON VANILLA EXTRACT
ONE 9-INCH PIE SHELL, UNBAKED
⅓ CUP BUTTER
½ CUP BROWN SUGAR
¾ CUP ALL-PURPOSE FLOUR

Preheat oven to 425° F.

Mix together gooseberries, 2 tablespoons flour, egg, granulated sugar, and vanilla, and place in pie shell.

Make a crumb mixture with butter, brown sugar, and ¾ cup flour. Sprinkle on top of gooseberries. Bake for 5 minutes. Reduce heat to 350° F. and bake 30 minutes more.

Mrs. Henry J. Shrock, Jamesport, MO

MULBERRY CREAM PIE
Yield: 6 servings

▼▼▼▼▼▼▼▼▼▼▼▼▼▼▼▼▼▼▼▼▼

CRUST:

2½ CUPS GRAHAM CRACKER CRUMBS
½ CUP TOASTED, FINELY CHOPPED PECANS
¾ STICK MELTED BUTTER
3 TABLESPOONS SUGAR

FILLING:

2½ CUPS FRESH MULBERRIES
¾ CUP WATER
6 EGG YOLKS
2 CUPS WHIPPING CREAM
½ CUP SUGAR
2 TEASPOONS LEMON JUICE
1 ENVELOPE UNFLAVORED GELATIN
1 CUP TOASTED AND FINELY CHOPPED PECANS
(OPTIONAL)

Preheat oven to 350° F.

Combine graham cracker crumbs, ½ cup pecans, butter, and 3 tablespoons sugar in a bowl and mix well. Press into a 10-inch deep-dish pie pan. Bake for 10 minutes. Let cool.

Cook mulberries in water and let cool. Drain liquid and save. Combine egg yolks, 1 cup of reserved mulberry liquid, 1 cup whipping cream, and ½ cup sugar in a 2-quart saucepan. Cook, whisking constantly on medium heat until mixture thickens, about 8-10 minutes. Do *not* boil. Pour into a mixing bowl and add lemon juice. Beat until cool, about 5 minutes.

Combine ¼ cup of reserved mulberry liquid or water and gelatin in a saucepan on low heat and mix until gelatin is melted. Add ½ cup of the cooling egg mixture to gelatin and mix. Gradually add gelatin mixture to remaining egg mixture. Cool in the refrigerator.

Whip remaining 1 cup whipping cream until it forms peaks. Fold in cooled mulberries. Then fold whipping cream mixture into almost-set egg mixture. Pour into cooled crust. Sprinkle with toasted pecans, if desired. Return to refrigerator and chill until set. It is best to leave for 6-8 hours, or overnight.

Felicity Gatchell, Birmingham, AL

ELDERBERRY PIE

Yield: 6 servings

This recipe was handed down from Grandma Campbell, who was married in 1884. I loved it as a child and still bake it a couple times when the berries are in season each year. It has the simplicity of old-time cooking.

▼▼▼▼▼▼▼▼▼▼▼▼▼▼▼▼▼▼▼▼▼▼

PASTRY FOR TWO 9-INCH PIE CRUSTS
1 QUART ELDERBERRIES, STEMMED AND WASHED
1 CUP SUGAR
2 TABLESPOONS ALL-PURPOSE FLOUR
1 CUP HEAVY CREAM

Preheat oven to 375° F. Line a 9-inch pie pan with half the pastry. Fill with elderberries. Combine sugar and flour. Add cream and mix well. Pour cream mixture over elderberries and top with lattice crust. Bake about 40 minutes, or until crust is golden brown.

Wanda Rezac, Sidney, NE

AMERICAN PERSIMMON PIE

Yield: 6 servings

Use very ripe fruit (almost mushy) for sweetness.

▼▼▼▼▼▼▼▼▼▼▼▼▼▼▼▼▼▼▼▼▼▼

2 CUPS PERSIMMON PULP
1 EGG, BEATEN
1 CUP MILK
½ CUP SUGAR
1 TABLESPOON CORNSTARCH
DASH SALT
PASTRY FOR ONE 9-INCH PIE CRUST

Preheat oven to 450° F.

Peel and press persimmons through colander. Mix pulp with egg and milk. Mix all dry ingredients together and add to pulp mixture. Pour mixture into a 9-inch pie pan lined with pastry. Bake for 10 minutes. Reduce heat to 350° F. and bake for 50-60 minutes more.

Merle R. Hudgins, Hungerford, TX

Mixed Fruit Pies

FRUIT PIZZA
Yield: 6 servings

▼▼▼▼▼▼▼▼▼▼▼▼▼▼▼▼▼▼▼▼▼▼

Sugar cookie recipe
8 ounces cream cheese
½ cup sugar
1 teaspoon vanilla extract
Approximately 4 cups *total* of sliced peaches, pineapple chunks, mandarin oranges, seedless grapes, sliced strawberries, sliced bananas (dipped in lemon juice to prevent darkening), sliced kiwi, sliced plums, or any kind of fruit you like
1½ cups fruit juice
2 tablespoons Minute Tapioca
⅓ cup sugar

Make your favorite sugar cookie recipe. Press the cookie dough in a greased pizza pan and bake. Cream together cream cheese, ½ cup sugar, and vanilla. Spread creamed mixture over cooled sugar cookie base.

Mix together approximately 4 cups of various fruits (or more, depending on the size of pizza pan) and pile on top of cream cheese mixture.

Mix together fruit juice, tapioca, and ⅓ cup sugar (or more if you like it sweeter). Cook on top of stove, stirring constantly until thick and clear. Cool. Pour over fruit, making sure all fruit has some of this mixture covering it. Refrigerate. Pizza will keep for two days.

Pauline Dawson, Ewing, MO

KANSAS MIXED FRUIT PIE

Yield: 6-8 servings

I was raised in Morrowville, Washington County, Kansas, until 14 years of age, during the 1930s— the Depression and the drought years. The fruits in this pie recipe were about all we could raise. The combination is very tasty and I still make it.

▼▼▼▼▼▼▼▼▼▼▼▼▼▼▼▼▼▼▼▼

1 CUP STEMMED GOOSEBERRIES

1 CUP PITTED PIE CHERRIES

1 CUP DICED RHUBARB

1 CUP MULBERRIES, IF AVAILABLE, OR 1 ADDITIONAL CUP OF ANY OF THE ABOVE FRUITS, ALONE OR IN COMBINATION, TO MAKE A TOTAL OF 4 CUPS OF FRUIT

1 CUP SUGAR

2 TABLESPOONS ALL-PURPOSE FLOUR

1 TABLESPOON CORNSTARCH

2 TABLESPOONS TAPIOCA

2 TEASPOONS BUTTER OR MARGARINE

PASTRY FOR TWO 10-INCH PIE CRUSTS

Preheat oven to 350° F.

Mix the 4 cups of fruit together. Add the sugar, flour, cornstarch, tapioca, and butter. Toss carefully to mix. Heat in a microwave oven for 2 minutes on HIGH, or a few minutes on top of stove in a heavy kettle, to melt butter and mix lightly. Place in a pastry-lined 10-inch pie plate. Put lattice, or any design, pastry on top. Bake for 30 minutes or until browned on top. Cool before eating. Top with ice cream, if desired.

Mildred (Nutsch) Chojnacky, Jerome, ID

A "WHAT'S THIS" BERRY PIE
Yield: 6 servings

I considered it a privilege to grow up in the country and watch my mother use what we had in the garden to feed the threshing crews each summer— and how they loved her cooking and desserts. She was famous and never gave it a thought as she prepared meals over a hot woodstove. I cherish her recipes.

▼▼▼▼▼▼▼▼▼▼▼▼▼▼▼▼▼▼▼▼▼▼▼

1 CUP BLUEBERRIES
1 CUP RASPBERRIES
2 CUPS MARION BLACKBERRIES, OR YOUR CHOICE
1½ CUPS SUGAR
⅓ CUP ALL-PURPOSE FLOUR
½ TEASPOON CINNAMON
PASTRY FOR TWO 9-INCH PIE CRUSTS
1½ TABLESPOONS BUTTER
COLD WATER
SUGAR

Preheat oven to 350° F.

Put berries in a large bowl. Mix together sugar, flour, and cinnamon. Sprinkle this over berries. Gently fold together.

Lightly grease a 9-inch pie pan. Roll out pastry to fit pan. Pour filling into crust. Dot with butter. Place second crust on top and cut slits for steam vents. Brush top crust with cold water and sprinkle with sugar. Bake for about 50 minutes or until bubbly.

Muriel Looney, Eugene, OR

MY GRANNY'S BERRY CREAM PIE

Yield: 6-8 servings

My Grandmother (Alice Reber) used to make this pie when I was a child in northern Michigan. When I began baking pies, at about age 12, it became one of my favorites to make, as well as to eat. When I was a child, we used the tiny wild huckleberries that grew in the pine woods, or wild blackberries or June-berries and we always used fresh cream from our milk cow. Now I find that buttermilk makes a tasty and healthier substitute.

▼▼▼▼▼▼▼▼▼▼▼▼▼▼▼▼▼▼▼▼▼

3 CUPS FRESH OR DRY-FROZEN BLUEBERRIES (OR SUBSTITUTE YOUR OWN FAVORITE: BLACKBERRY, RASPBERRY, SWEET CHERRY, OR MULBERRY)

ONE 9-INCH PIE SHELL, UNBAKED

1 CUP SUGAR

¼ CUP ALL-PURPOSE FLOUR

⅛ TEASPOON SALT

¾ CUP CREAM (OR SUBSTITUTE BUTTERMILK, IF YOU ARE CHOLESTEROL-CONSCIOUS)

Preheat oven to 425° F. Pour berries into pie shell. Stir together sugar, flour, and salt. Stir in cream. Pour cream mixture over berries. Bake for 10 minutes. Reduce heat to 350° F. and bake for approximately 45 minutes more or until bubbly near center of pie. Serve slightly warm or cool.

Betty Hofstetter, Millersburg, OH

APPLE-PEAR FLAN

Yield: 6 servings

▼▼▼▼▼▼▼▼▼▼▼▼▼▼▼▼▼▼▼▼▼▼

CRUST:

1 CUP UNBLEACHED ALL-PURPOSE FLOUR

½ CUP CHILLED, SWEET BUTTER

1 TABLESPOON SUGAR

½ TEASPOON SALT

2-3 TABLESPOONS ICE WATER

FILLING:

2 LARGE PEARS

2 LARGE APPLES

4 TABLESPOONS SUGAR

4 TABLESPOONS SWEET BUTTER

¼ CUP APRICOT JELLY

2 TABLESPOONS WATER

Combine flour, butter, 1 tablespoon sugar, and salt. Mix well with a fork until mixture has the consistency of cornmeal. Add ice water and form dough into a ball. Refrigerate dough for 1 hour. Roll dough into a circle and line a 9-inch tart pan. Put tart crust in freezer while preparing filling.

Preheat oven to 400° F. Peel, halve, and core pears and apples. Slice pears and apples thinly lengthwise, holding pears and apples to retain shape. Fill tart shell with fruit to create a flower design. Sprinkle with 4 tablespoons sugar and dot with butter. Bake for 50-60 minutes or until golden brown.

Prepare glaze by heating apricot jelly and water in a small saucepan and stirring until smooth. Brush glaze on warm tart and serve immediately or gently reheat before serving.

Joan Downs, Davisburg, MI

FRESH FRUIT COBBLER

Yield: 6 servings

▼▼▼▼▼▼▼▼▼▼▼▼▼▼▼▼▼▼▼

3 CUPS FRESH FRUIT (APPLES, PEACHES, BLUEBERRIES, OR PEARS)
1¾ CUPS SUGAR
½ CUP MILK
¼ TEASPOON SALT
3 TABLESPOONS BUTTER
1 CUP ALL-PURPOSE FLOUR
1 TEASPOON BAKING POWDER
1 CUP BOILING WATER
1 TABLESPOON CORNSTARCH

Preheat oven to 350° F. Place fruit in bottom of a 9" x 9" baking pan. Mix together ¾ cup sugar, milk, salt, unmelted butter, flour, and baking powder. Pour over fruit. Combine remaining sugar, water, and cornstarch. Pour over mixture in pan. Bake for 50-60 minutes.

Jo Ann Pussehl, Eminence, MO

DEEP-DISH MIXED BERRY CRISP

Yield: 12 servings

▼▼▼▼▼▼▼▼▼▼▼▼▼▼▼▼▼▼▼▼▼

FILLING:

2 CUPS FRESH RASPBERRIES (OR FROZEN AND THAWED)

4 CUPS FRESH STRAWBERRIES (OR FROZEN AND THAWED)

½ CUP CORNSTARCH

½ TEASPOON GROUND CLOVES

¼ TEASPOON CINNAMON

5 CUPS ASSORTED BERRIES: RASPBERRIES, STRAWBERRIES, BLACKBERRIES, AND BLUEBERRIES

½ CUP HONEY

TOPPING:

1 CUP ROLLED OATS

½ CUP WHOLE WHEAT FLOUR

½ CUP WHEAT GERM

½ CUP BROWN SUGAR

2 TEASPOONS CINNAMON

¼ CUP CHOPPED WALNUTS

½ CUP COLD BUTTER

Preheat oven to 350° F. Lightly oil a 2½-quart glass casserole or soufflé dish.

For filling, in a 4-quart saucepan combine raspberries and strawberries with cornstarch. Heat to boiling, stirring until sauce is thick and clear. Stir in cloves and cinnamon. Fold 5 cups berries into hot berry sauce. Add honey and spoon sauce into oiled casserole.

Combine topping ingredients, cutting in butter. Sprinkle topping over berries. Place casserole on rimmed baking sheet. Bake for 25-30 minutes.

Marsha Wilson, Jefferson City, MO

INDEX

▼▼